AAT

Qualifications and Credit Framework (QCF)

LEVEL 3 DIPLOMA IN ACCOUNTING

COMBINED TEXT AND QUESTION BANK

Indirect Tax

2011 Edition

Second edition July 2011

Printed text ISBN 9780 7517 9733 6

British Library Cataloguing-in-Publication Data
A catalogue record for this book is available from the British
Library

Published by

BPP Learning Media Ltd
BPP House
Aldine Place
London
W12 8AA

www.bpp.com/learningmedia

Printed in the United Kingdom

We are grateful to the AAT for permission to reproduce the
sample assessment and the reference material for the AAT
assessment of Indirect Tax. The answers to the sample assessment
have been published by the AAT. All other answers have been
prepared by BPP Learning Media Ltd.

CONTENTS

A NOTE ABOUT COPYRIGHT

Dear Customer

What does the little © mean and why does it matter?

Your market-leading BPP books, course materials and e-learning materials do not write and update themselves. People write them: on their own behalf or as employees of an organisation that invests in this activity. Copyright law protects their livelihoods. It does so by creating rights over the use of the content.

Breach of copyright is a form of theft – as well as being a criminal offence in some jurisdictions, it is potentially a serious breach of professional ethics.

With current technology, things might seem a bit hazy but, basically, without the express permission of BPP Learning Media:

- Photocopying our materials is a breach of copyright

- Scanning, ripcasting or conversion of our digital materials into different file formats, uploading them to facebook or emailing them to your friends is a breach of copyright

You can, of course, sell your books, in the form in which you have bought them – once you have finished with them. (Is this fair to your fellow students? We update for a reason.)

And what about outside the UK? BPP Learning Media strives to make our materials available at prices students can afford by local printing arrangements, pricing policies and partnerships which are clearly listed on our website. A tiny minority ignore this and indulge in criminal activity by illegally photocopying our material or supporting organisations that do. If they act illegally and unethically in one area, can you really trust them?

INTRODUCTION

Since 1 July 2010 the AAT's assessments have fallen within the **Qualifications and Credit Framework** and most papers are now assessed by way of an on demand **computer based assessment**. BPP Learning Media has reacted to this change by investing heavily to produce new ground breaking market leading resources. In particular, our **new suite of online resources** ensures that you are prepared for online testing by means of an online environment where tasks mimic the style of the AAT's assessment tasks.

The first part of this **Combined Text and Question Bank** covers all the knowledge and understanding needed by you, with numerous illustrations of 'how it works', practical examples and tasks for you to use to consolidate your learning. The majority of tasks within the texts have been written in an interactive style that reflects the style of the online tasks the AAT will set. Texts are available in our traditional paper format and, in addition, as E-books which can be downloaded to your PC or laptop.

At the back of this **Combined Text and Question Bank** there are additional learning questions corresponding back to the Text, plus the AAT's sample assessment and a number of other full practice assessments. Full answers to all questions and assessments, prepared by BPP Learning Media Ltd, are included. Our question banks are also available in an online environment which mimics the AAT's testing environment. This enables you to familiarise yourself with the environment in which you will be tested

BPP's range of resources available for the Indirect Tax Assessment also includes:

- **Passcards,** which are handy pocket sized revision tools designed to fit in a handbag or briefcase to enable students to revise anywhere at anytime. All major points are covered in the passcards which have been designed to assist you in consolidating knowledge

- **Workbooks,** which have been designed to cover the units that are assessed by way of project/case study. The workbooks contain many practical tasks to assist in the learning process and also a sample assessment or project to work through.

- **Lecturers' resources**, providing a further bank of tasks, answers and full practice assessments for classroom use, available separately only to lecturers whose colleges adopt BPP Learning Media material. The lecturers resources are available in both paper format and online in E format.

This Combined Text and Question Bank for Indirect Tax has been written specifically to ensure comprehensive yet concise coverage of the AAT's learning outcomes and assessment criteria. It is fully up to date as at June 2011. It reflects the AAT's unit guide and the sample assessment provided by the AAT, and also incorporates the reference material that is available within the live assessment.

Each chapter contains:

- clear, step by step explanation of the topic

- logical progression and linking from one chapter to the next

- numerous illustrations of 'how it works'

- interactive tasks within the text of the chapter itself, with answers at the back of the book. In general, these tasks have been written in the interactive form that students will see in their real assessments

- test your learning questions of varying complexity, again with answers supplied at the back of the book. In general these test questions have been written in the interactive form that students will see in their real assessments

The Question Bank at the back contains these key features:

- graded tasks corresponding to each chapter of the Text. Some tasks are designed for learning purposes, others are of assessment standard

- the AAT's sample assessment and answers for Indirect tax and further practice assessments

The emphasis in all tasks and assessments is on the practical application of the skills acquired.

If you have any comments about this book, please e-mail ambercottrell@bpp.com or write to Amber Cottrell, Tax Publishing Manager, BPP Learning Media Ltd, BPP House, Aldine Place, London W12 8AA.

A NOTE ABOUT VAT

There was a change in the standard rate of VAT from 17.5% to 20% on 4 January 2011. In assessments from 1 September 2011 you should use a standard rate of 20%.

ASSESSMENT STRATEGY

Indirect Tax (ITX) is the only tax assessment at level 3.

ITX is a 90 minute assessment. The assessment material will normally be provided by the AAT, delivered online and assessed locally. Within the learning objectives outlined below, the AAT state that emphasis is not being placed so much on recalling information, more on awareness and understanding of how to apply it. Therefore detailed reference material is available during the assessment to refer to where necessary. A copy of this material is provided at the back of this text.

The ITX assessment consists of eight tasks, five in Section 1 and three in Section 2.

Section 1 will comprise five short-answer tasks assessing the learner's knowledge of the principles of VAT and their ability to understand and interpret VAT guidance given to them. Some simple calculations will be required. A number of the tasks will be multiple-choice or true/false statements.

Section 2 will comprise three tasks. These will focus on the completion of VAT returns, and communication skills. Information will need to be extracted from accounting systems for the first two tasks, followed by a short piece of communication to an internal or external person for the final task.

Competency

Learners will be required to demonstrate competence in both sections of the assessment. For the purpose of assessment the competency level for AAT assessment is set at 70 per cent. The level descriptor in the table below describes the ability and skills students at this level must successfully demonstrate to achieve competence.

QCF Level descriptor	Summary
	Achievement at level 3 reflects the ability to identify and use relevant understanding, methods and skills to complete tasks and address problems that, while well defined, have a measure of complexity. It includes taking responsibility for initiating and completing tasks and procedures as well as exercising autonomy and judgement within limited parameters. It also reflects awareness of different perspectives or approaches within an area of study or work.
	Knowledge and understanding
	▪ Use factual, procedural and theoretical understanding to complete tasks and address problems that, while well defined, may be complex and non-routine
	▪ Interpret and evaluate relevant information and ideas
	▪ Be aware of the nature of the area of study or work
	▪ Have awareness of different perspectives or approaches within the area of study or work
	Application and action
	▪ Address problems that, while well defined, may be complex and non routine
	▪ Identify, select and use appropriate skills, methods and procedures
	▪ Use appropriate investigation to inform actions
	▪ Review how effective methods and actions have been
	Autonomy and accountability
	▪ Take responsibility for initiating and completing tasks and procedures, including, where relevant, responsibility for supervising or guiding others
	▪ Exercise autonomy and judgement within limited parameters

AAT UNIT GUIDE

Indirect Tax

Introduction

Please read this in conjunction with the standards for the unit.

Successful completion of this AAT learning and assessment area will result in the award of two QCF units:

- Preparing and completing VAT returns (skills)
- Principles of VAT (knowledge)

The purpose of the unit

The unit is designed to ensure that learners can understand basic VAT regulations, accurately complete VAT returns, and communicate VAT information to relevant people. As VAT is subject to specific and detailed regulations, the learner should be able to seek guidance from relevant sources, process what is found and communicate this to others.

Learning objectives

After successful completion of this unit, the learner will be able to deal with the most commonly occurring VAT issues in a business. Although some basic knowledge will be expected, the emphasis is not so much on recall as on awareness and understanding. The learner will be aware that regulations exist and know how to find the information to ensure that the business complies with the regulations and avoids surcharges and penalties. The learner will be able to extract information from the relevant source and, using their knowledge and understanding, apply the rules to the given situations.

Learners will be aware of registration requirements and the existence of a variety of schemes with different requirements to suit businesses with different needs. They will be able to calculate VAT correctly and use an accounting system to extract the figures required to complete the VAT return.

They will also be aware of special circumstances that require particular attention and be able to deal with errors and changes in the VAT rate, as well as being able to communicate on VAT issues with people inside and outside the business.

Learning outcomes

There are two QCF units involved. Each is divided into component learning outcomes, which in turn comprise a number of assessment criteria.

QCF Unit	Learning Outcome	Assessment Criteria	Covered in Chapters
Preparing and completing VAT returns (skills)	Complete VAT returns accurately and in a timely manner	Correctly identify and extract relevant data for a specific period from the accounting system	**2,3,5-8**
		Calculate accurately relevant inputs and outputs:	
		▪ standard supplies	
		▪ exempt supplies	
		▪ zero rated supplies	
		▪ imports	
		▪ exports	
		Calculate accurately the VAT due to, or from, the relevant tax authority	
		Make adjustments and declarations for any errors or omissions identified in previous VAT periods	
		Complete accurately and submit a VAT return within the statutory time limits along with any associated payments	
	Communicate VAT information	Inform managers of the impact that the VAT payment may have on the company cash flow and financial forecasts	**6,7,9**
		Advise relevant people of the impact that any changes in VAT legislation, including the VAT rate, would have on the organisation's recording systems	
		Communicate effectively with the relevant tax authority when seeking guidance	

QCF Unit	Learning Outcome	Assessment Criteria	Covered in Chapters
Principles of VAT (knowledge)	Understand VAT regulations	Identify sources of information on VAT	**1-5,7,8**
		Explain the relationship between the organisation and the relevant government authority	
		Explain the VAT registration requirements	
		Identify the information that must be included on business documentation of VAT-registered businesses	
		Recognise different types of inputs and outputs	
		Identify how different types of supply are classified for VAT purposes:	
		■ standard supplies	
		■ exempt supplies	
		■ zero rated supplies	
		■ imports	
		■ exports	
		Explain the requirements and the frequency of reporting for the following VAT schemes:	
		■ annual accounting	
		■ cash accounting	
		■ flat rate	
		■ standard	
		Recognise the implications and penalties for the organisation resulting from failure to abide by VAT regulations including the late submission of VAT returns	

Delivery guidance: Preparing and completing VAT returns

1. **Complete VAT returns accurately and in a timely manner**

   1.1 Correctly identify and extract relevant data for a specific period from the accounting system

   - Learners will be expected to extract relevant net and VAT figures from the accounting system

     - Sales day book

     - Purchases day book

     - Cash book

     - Petty cash book

     - Journal

     - General ledger accounts for sales, purchases, input VAT, output VAT

   1.2 Calculate accurately relevant inputs and outputs

   - Using the basic rounding rule (rounding down total VAT to the nearest penny) calculate correctly the VAT and input and output figures for

     - Standard supplies

     - Exempt supplies

     - Zero-rated supplies

     - Imports

     - Exports

     - The detailed rounding rules based on lines of goods and services and tax per unit or article are not required

   - *No knowledge required of the detail of which specific items fall into each category of standard, exempt and zero-rated.*

   - Be able to calculate VAT from net sales amounts at different rates of VAT, including cases when a settlement discount is offered.

   - Be able to calculate the amount of VAT arising when given either the gross amount or the net amount of a supply.

   - Know in broad terms how imports and exports, and their related VAT, are treated on a VAT return, including the significance of the EC. (no knowledge of Intrastate returns is expected)

   - Know that exports are normally zero-rated.

- Correctly account for VAT on business entertainment, sales and purchases of cars and vans and deposits or advance payments.

- Be aware of fuel scale charges and the effect on the total VAT payable/reclaimable (but no calculations).

1.3 Calculate accurately the VAT due to, or from, the relevant tax authority In respect of

- Transactions in the current period
- Adjustments for bad debt relief

1.4 Make adjustments and declarations for any errors or omissions identified in previous VAT periods

- The errors or omissions will be given

- Identify whether the error or omission can be corrected on the current VAT return by identifying the threshold at which errors must be declared and the timescale during which corrections can be made

- Apply the correct treatment

- How to report an error that cannot be corrected on the current VAT return.

1.5 Complete accurately and submit a VAT return within the statutory time limits along with any associated payments

- Knowledge of what the time limits are, including those relating to non-standard schemes

- Accurate calculation of the VAT due to, or from, HMRC, both in respect of transactions in the current period and also in relation to errors and omissions identified from previous periods

    - Transactions include sales and purchase invoices and credits, cash payments and receipts, petty cash payments

- Complete a VAT return (VAT 100, paper or online version); Boxes 1 to 9.

- Be aware that most businesses will need to submit the VAT return and pay online.

- Understand that the balance on the VAT control account should agree to the figure on the VAT return and provide explanations for any difference.

2 **Communicate VAT information**

2.1 Inform managers of the impact that the VAT payment may have on the company cash flow and financial forecasts

- Know the time limits within which payment must be made under various schemes

- Communicate this via standard communication methods such as emails.

2.2 Advise relevant people of the impact that any changes in VAT legislation, including the VAT rate, would have on the organisation's recording systems

- Basic understanding of the implication of a change in the VAT rate on the organisation using either manual or computerised systems

- Basic understanding of who would need to be informed and why

- Advise relevant people by email or other appropriate means

2.3 Communicate effectively with the relevant tax authority when seeking guidance

- Using letters

Delivery guidance: Principles of VAT

1 **Understand VAT regulations**

1.1 Identify sources of information on VAT

- Extract information from relevant sources

1.2 Explain the relationship between the organisation and the relevant government authority

- Understanding that

    - HMRC is a government body entitled to require organisations to comply with VAT regulations in relation to registration, record keeping, submission of returns etc

    - VAT is a tax on consumer expenditure

    - It is advisable to get written confirmation from HMRC about issues on which doubt may arise as to the correct treatment

    - HMRC are entitled to inspect VAT records during control visits (no further detail of control visits is expected)

1.3 Explain the VAT registration requirements

- The registration threshold and when registration becomes compulsory

- Circumstances in which voluntary registration may be beneficial to the business

- Awareness of circumstances when deregistration may be appropriate, and the de-registration threshold

- Which records must be kept and for how long

1.4 Identify the information that must be included on business documentation of VAT-registered businesses

- And by implication information that is not required

- Including less detailed VAT invoices and VAT receipts, and invoicing for zero-rated and exempt supplies

- Tax points – basic and actual, including where payment is in advance of supply or invoice is after the supply, but not continuous supply or goods on sale or return. The importance of tax points for determining eligibility for schemes, correct rate of VAT, and including figures on the VAT return

- Time limits for VAT invoices including the 14-day rule

- Rounding rules

1.5 Recognise different types of inputs and outputs

- What are inputs and outputs, and what are input and output tax?

- How to treat different types of inputs and outputs in preparing a VAT return, including

  - Pro forma invoices

- the implication of the difference between zero-rated and exempt supplies with respect to reclaiming input VAT should be recognised

1.6 Identify how different types of supply are classified for VAT purposes

- Standard supplies

- Exempt supplies

- Zero-rated supplies

- Imports

- Exports

- *No knowledge required of the detail of which specific items fall into each category*

- The basics of partial exemption, including an awareness of the de minimus limit that enables full recovery of input VAT for businesses with mixed exempt and taxable supplies. Calculations will not be required.

1.7 Explain the requirements and the frequency of reporting for the following VAT schemes

- Annual accounting

- Cash accounting

- Flat-rate scheme

- Standard scheme

- Be able to explain in broad terms the way in which each scheme works and the situations in which an organisation would be likely to use one.

- Know the effect of each scheme on the frequency of VAT reporting and payments.

1.8 Recognise the implications and penalties for the organisation resulting from failure to abide by VAT regulations including the late submission of VAT returns

- The main principles of the enforcement regime, but not the fine detail.

    - What triggers a surcharge liability notice. Will not be expected to know how the amount of the surcharge is calculated, or what happens if a further default arises in the surcharge period, etc

    - Penalties – awareness of fines and that evasion of VAT is a criminal offence

chapter 1:
THE VAT SYSTEM

chapter coverage 📖

Although you will have come across Value Added Tax (VAT) in your earlier studies, we begin this chapter with a reminder of how the VAT system works. We then consider some of the more detailed areas you will meet when dealing with and accounting for VAT. The topics covered are:

✍ Value Added Tax - The system

   – HM Revenue and Customs' website

   – The VAT Guide

✍ Operation of Value Added Tax

✍ VAT and accounting records

   – Information that must be recorded

   – Sales records

   – Purchases and expenses records

VALUE ADDED TAX – THE SYSTEM

What is VAT?

Value Added Tax (VAT) is essentially a sales tax – it is a tax on spending and is an important source of revenue for the government. Similar forms of sales tax are also charged in many other countries, although you only need to be aware of the system in the UK.

VAT regulation

The VAT system in the UK is administered by HM Revenue & Customs (HMRC). This government body is entitled to require organisations to comply with VAT regulations.

VAT regulations, including rates and allowances, are contained in legislation. In the assessment you will be provided with reference material that will contain the rates and allowances that you will need in the assessment. A copy of the reference material provided is included at the back of this Text.

In addition to the legislation, advice about VAT rules and regulations is given in HMRC guidance.

Increasingly, HMRC issues advice notes and guidance online via its website www.hmrc.gov.uk. This is updated far more frequently than the paper publications and you should get used to searching the HMRC website in preference to relying on hard copy publications.

However, HMRC also issues VAT 700 "The VAT Guide", which provides a business with all the information it needs about accounting for, recording and paying over VAT. The VAT Guide can be sent to you free of charge by simply contacting the VAT Helpline. Alternatively, you can access it at HMRC's website. You are not expected to know all of the details of The VAT Guide but the main elements will be covered throughout this Text.

HMRC does not update The VAT Guide on a regular basis, and it may be necessary to look at the website for other guidance to ensure that you are looking at the most up-to-date information.

The Business Link website contains some VAT reference material that is kept more up to date and can be found at http://www.businesslink.gov.uk/bdotg/action/layer?r.s=tl&r.l1=1073858808&r.lc=en&topicId=1083126673

Before we begin to look at how the VAT system works, we will start with a brief reminder of the details of how a business must record and account for VAT.

OPERATION OF VALUE ADDED TAX

If the sales of a business exceed a certain amount for a year, then a business must register for VAT. They then have a VAT registration number which must be included on invoices and other business documents.

This means that the business must charge its customers VAT on all of its taxable supplies or sales, normally at the standard rate of 20%. This is known as OUTPUT VAT or OUTPUT TAX (VAT on goods going 'OUT' of the business).

There is, however, a benefit in that the VAT that the business pays (when buying from suppliers or paying expenses) can be recovered back from HMRC. This is known as INPUT VAT or INPUT TAX (VAT on goods coming 'IN' to the business).

Every three months (usually) the business must complete a VAT return (see later in this Text) showing the output and input VAT. The business effectively acts as an agent for HMRC. In this way

- OUTPUT VAT charged to customers is paid over to HMRC, and
- INPUT VAT charged to the business by suppliers is reclaimed from HMRC

The excess of output VAT over input VAT must be paid to HMRC with the VAT return. However, if the input VAT exceeds the output VAT then a refund is due from HMRC (this will be dealt with in detail later in this Text).

HOW IT WORKS

Let's follow a simple manufacturing process through the VAT payment process.

Business	Transaction		HMRC VAT due
Supplier of wood	Sells wood to table manufacturer for £160 + VAT of £32		
	Sale value	£160	
	Output VAT	£32	£32
Table manufacturer	Purchases wood from supplier for £160 + VAT of £32		
	Sells table to retailer for £280 + VAT of £56		
	Sale value	£280	
	Purchases value	£160	
	Output VAT – Input VAT		
	(£56 – £32)	£24	£24
Retailer	Purchases table from manufacturer for £280 + VAT of £56		
	Sells table to customer for £360 + VAT of £72		
	Sale value	£360	
	Purchases value	£280	
	Output VAT – Input VAT		
	(£72 – £56)	£16	£16
Customer	Purchases table for £360 + VAT of £72		
	Pays retailer (£360 + £72)	£432	£0
Total VAT paid to HMRC			£72

Note that it is the final customer (consumer) – often a member of the general public - who suffers the cost of the VAT. The table cost him £432 not £360, but the customer does not have to pay the VAT to HMRC as this has already been done throughout the chain of manufacture and sale.

Task 1

Business A sells goods to Business B for £1,000 plus £200 of VAT. Which business treats the VAT as input tax and which treats it as output tax?

	Input tax ✓	Output tax ✓
Business A		✓
Business B	✓	

VAT AND ACCOUNTING RECORDS

VAT affects most of the everyday transactions of a business. A VAT-registered business will charge VAT on its sales and will pay VAT on its purchases and expense payments. These sales, purchases and expenses may be on credit or they may be for cash.

The VAT Guide sets out in detail the records that should be kept by a VAT-registered business. The reference material provided in the assessment also lists these records. Each individual business accounting system will be different but, in general terms, you must keep records of all taxable goods and services which you receive or supply. In practice, you must also be able to distinguish between supplies that are

- standard-rated (20%)
- reduced rate (5%)
- zero-rated (0%) and
- exempt supplies (no VAT).

However in the assessment you will be told to which category a supply belongs. These will all be considered in more detail later in the Text.

The records must be kept up-to-date in order that, each quarter, the correct amount of VAT due to or from HMRC can be calculated and entered onto the VAT return. Whatever method the business uses to keep these records, they must be kept in such a way that HMRC officers can easily check that the figures on the VAT returns are correct.

Information that must be recorded

The information that must be kept by all businesses in order to be able to correctly calculate the VAT due includes the following:

- Details of all standard-rated, reduced-rate, zero-rated and exempt goods or services the business received

- Details of all standard-rated, reduced-rate, zero-rated and exempt supplies made by the business

- Details of all trade within the European Union

- Details of all trade outside the EU

HMRC requires that these records should normally be kept for six years.

HMRC has an entitlement to inspect a taxpayer's VAT records at any time.

Sales (revenue) records

In order to be able to determine the correct total for the **output VAT** of a business, the following detailed records of all sales made must be kept:

SALES INVOICES issued to customers. An exception to this is when retailers issue less detailed invoices (for items under £250 inclusive of VAT)

CREDIT NOTES issued or DEBIT NOTES received for goods returned.

These detailed records are considered further in the next chapter.

The accounting records that most businesses keep in order to record their sales are the following:

Sales day book – this is a record of all the invoices sent out to credit customers showing the net amount of the sale, the VAT and the invoice total.

Sales returns day book – this is a record of all the credit notes sent out to credit customers or debit notes received from credit customers for returns and alterations to invoice amounts. Again, this will show the net amount of the credit/debit note, the VAT and the full value of the credit/debit note.

Cash receipts book – this records receipts from credit customers as well as other receipts for cash sales. You will remember from your accounting studies that the amount to be recorded for the receipts from credit customers is the full invoice total – the VAT does not need to be analysed here as this has already been done in the sales day book. However, where cash sales are made and VAT has been charged on the sale then the cash receipts book should show the net amount of the sale, the VAT and the final total.

Task 2

A business issues a credit note to a customer. Which of the following statements is correct?

	✓
Input tax will increase	
Input tax will decrease	
Output tax will increase	
Output tax will decrease	

Purchases and expenses records

When a business receives invoices for purchases or expenses then these must all be kept. The business must keep purchase invoices for goods and services received that are not only standard-rated supplies but also those that are zero-rated and exempt. A business can only claim **input VAT** if they have a valid VAT invoice. We will determine what a valid VAT invoice is in the next chapter.

PURCHASES DAY BOOK – this is a record of all the invoices received from credit suppliers showing the net amount of the supply, the VAT and the invoice total.

PURCHASES RETURNS DAY BOOK – this is a record of all of the credit notes received by the business and any debit notes issued. Again, these will be analysed to show the net amount of the credit, any VAT and the total of the credit/debit note.

CASH PAYMENTS BOOK – this is a record of all of the payments made by the business. The payments to credit suppliers are recorded as the total payment with no analysis of the VAT element as this has already been analysed out in the purchases day book. However, all other payments for goods or expenses that have attracted VAT should be recorded as the net amount, the VAT and the full amount of the payment.

Petty cash records

When a business makes minor payments, for example small items of office stationery, or purchases of tea and coffee for staff, money is taken out of the petty cash box. This is evidenced by a **petty cash voucher**. The petty cash voucher must be retained by the business and contains details of the expense incurred and any VAT charged. It is usual for the purchase invoice to be attached to the petty cash voucher. You can only claim the input VAT if you have the valid VAT invoice, and not just the petty cash voucher.

Petty cash book – this is a record of all of the payments made by the business. Details of petty cash vouchers will be recorded in the **petty cash payments BOOK**.

The journal

The **journal** is the book of prime entry for non-standard transactions such as payroll transactions, writing off irrecoverable (bad) debts and correcting errors, that do not fall into any of the day books mentioned above. Some of the journal entries may have an impact on VAT such as the writing off of an irrecoverable debt relating to a standard rated supply.

A VAT account

This is a separate account to record the VAT payable (output tax) and VAT deductible (input tax) to HMRC by the business. It provides a link between the business accounts and the VAT return.

This account will be considered further throughout this Text.

Much of the information covered in this chapter is available to view throughout the live assessment within the reference material. You should familiarise yourself with this document (included at the back of this Text) and practise using it when attempting any Tasks.

CHAPTER OVERVIEW

- The VAT system is administered by HM Revenue and Customs, which issues VAT 700 "The VAT Guide" and various other advice notes and guidance via its website

- The ultimate consumer bears the cost of the VAT

- All VAT-registered persons must keep full records of the details of all trade both within the EU and outside the EU and details of all standard-rated, zero-rated and exempt goods and services both purchased and sold.

- These records should normally be kept for six years and must be made available to an HMRC officer if required

- Copies of sales invoices must be kept and the main accounting records for sales will be the sales day book, sales returns day book and the cash book

- All invoices for purchases and expenses must be kept otherwise the input VAT cannot be reclaimed – the main accounting records for purchases and expenses are the purchases day book, the purchases returns day book and the cash book

- The VAT account records the VAT payable and deductible by the business and is a link between the business records and the VAT return

Keywords

Output VAT or Output tax – VAT on the sale of goods and the provision of services. This is paid by the business to HMRC

Input VAT or Input tax – VAT on the purchases of goods and payment of expenses. This is reclaimed by the business from HMRC, provided there is a valid VAT invoice

Sales day book – A record of all invoices sent to credit customers

Sales returns day book – A record of all credit notes sent to credit customers

Cash receipts book – A record of all receipts of the business

Purchases day book – A record of all invoices received from credit suppliers

Purchases returns day book – A record of all credit notes received from suppliers

Cash payments book – A record of all payments made by the business

TEST YOUR LEARNING

Test 1

Which organisation administers VAT in the UK? Tick the relevant box below.

	✓
HM Customs and Excise	
Inland Revenue	
HM Revenue and Customs	
HM Treasury	

Test 2

Choose which ONE of the following statements is correct. Tick the relevant box below.

	✓
Output VAT is the VAT charged by a supplier on the sales that are made by his business. Output VAT is collected by the supplier and paid over to HMRC.	
Output VAT is the VAT suffered by the purchaser of the goods which will be reclaimed from HMRC if the purchaser is VAT registered and a valid VAT invoice is held.	

Test 3

Explain how it is that the final consumer pays the full amount of VAT to the seller but never pays any money to HMRC.

Test 4

How long does HMRC usually require relevant documents to be kept? Tick the relevant box below.

	✓
1 year	
2 years	
6 years	
20 years	

chapter 2:
ACCOUNTING FOR VAT

chapter coverage 📖

In this chapter we focus on the detail to be included on various types of VAT invoice. We also look at how a business decides which tax period to include a transaction in and start to consider how records are entered in the VAT account. The topics covered are:

✍ VAT invoices

✍ Credit notes and debit notes

✍ Tax point

✍ VAT account

VAT INVOICES

If a business is registered for VAT and it makes a supply to another VAT-registered business, then it must send a VAT invoice within 30 days of the supply as shown below:

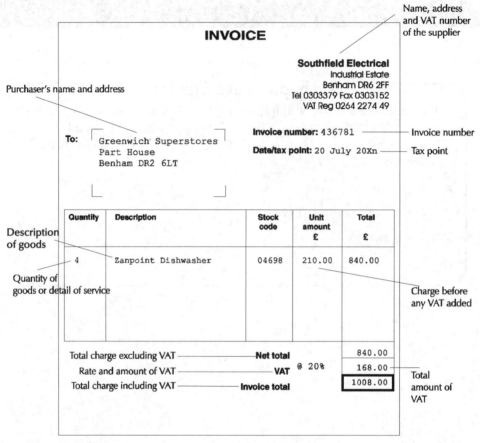

The items pointed out on the invoice above must be included on a valid VAT invoice, and are listed below:

- The supplier's name, address and registration number

- The date of issue, the tax point, if different (see later in the Text)

- An invoice number

- The name and address of the customer

- A description of the goods or services supplied, giving for each description the quantity, the unit price, the rate of VAT and the VAT exclusive amount

- The rate of any cash or settlement discount

- The total invoice price excluding VAT (with separate totals for zero-rated and exempt supplies)

- Each VAT rate applicable and the total amount of VAT

This list is included in the reference material provided within the assessment.

The business must keep a copy of the invoice.

The issuing of a VAT invoice for standard or reduced rate supplies by a business,

- increases the output VAT, and so
- increases the amount payable to HMRC by the business.

The receipt of a purchase invoice for standard or reduced rate supplies by a VAT-registered business,

- increases the input VAT, and so
- increases the amount to be reclaimed from HMRC by the business.

Task 1

Which three of the following items must be included on a valid VAT invoice?

	✓
Customer VAT registration number	
Supplier VAT registration number	
Total VAT-exclusive amount	
Total VAT amount	
Total VAT-inclusive amount	

Task 2

A purchase invoice for taxable supplies has just been processed. What will be the effect on VAT? Choose ONE answer.

	✓
Input tax will increase	
Input tax will decrease	
Output tax will increase	
Output tax will decrease	

Less detailed VAT invoice

If a business is in the retail trade then the customer should always be given a VAT invoice if so requested by the customer.

However, if the charge for the goods is less than £250, including VAT, then a LESS DETAILED VAT INVOICE (sometimes referred to as a simplified invoice) can be issued showing:

- Business name, address and VAT registration number

- The time of supply (tax point)

- A description of the goods or services supplied

- For each VAT rate applicable, the total amount payable including the VAT and the VAT rate charged.

In particular, note that no details relating to the customer, or VAT-exclusive amounts are required. Again, these details are listed on the reference material supplied in the assessment.

If credit cards are accepted, then a less detailed invoice can be created by adapting the sales voucher given to the customer. It must include the information listed above.

Suppliers do not need to keep copies of less detailed invoices issued, unless the customer has asked for a VAT invoice. A customer would need to keep a copy if they wanted to reclaim the input tax.

Pro forma invoice

A PRO FORMA INVOICE is often used in order to offer goods to a potential customer at a certain price and to invite the customer to send a payment in return for which the goods will be despatched. This is often the case when a business does not wish to sell on credit but instead needs payment up front before the goods are dispatched.

When the pro forma invoice is received by the potential customer it cannot be used by the customer as evidence to reclaim the VAT element. Therefore any pro forma invoice should be clearly marked "THIS IS NOT A VAT INVOICE".

If the customer does decide to buy the goods or sends payment then a proper VAT invoice must be issued. The customer can only reclaim input tax when they receive a proper VAT invoice.

Task 3

Decide whether the following statements are true or false. Tick the relevant boxes below.

	True ✓	False ✓
A 'less detailed' invoice can be used to reclaim input VAT		
A 'pro forma' invoice can be used to reclaim input VAT		

CREDIT NOTES AND DEBIT NOTES

VAT-registered business receiving returned goods from a customer

If a customer returns goods then it is customary to issue a CREDIT NOTE to reflect the value of these goods, including the VAT element. Alternatively, the original invoice can be cancelled and recovered, and a replacement invoice issued showing the correct amount of VAT; or the customer may issue a DEBIT NOTE which reflects the value of the goods returned and the VAT element.

Credit notes and debit notes can also be issued to correct errors that have been made on the original invoice.

If a VAT-registered business issues a credit note (or receives a debit note) for returned goods, it must record this in its accounting records and deduct the VAT from the amount of VAT payable on the next VAT return.

Therefore issuing a sales credit note,

- decreases the output VAT, and so
- decreases the amount payable to HMRC by the business.

Returning goods to a supplier

If goods are returned to a supplier then a business can obtain a credit note. Alternatively, the business can return the original invoice to the supplier and obtain a replacement invoice showing the correct amount of VAT; or the business may issue a debit note to the supplier which reflects the value of the goods returned and the VAT element.

If a VAT-registered business receives a credit note (or issues a debit note) for returning goods to the supplier it must record this in its accounting records and deduct the VAT from the amount of VAT reclaimable on the next VAT return.

The receipt of a purchase credit note by a VAT-registered business,

- decreases the input VAT, and so
- decreases the amount to be reclaimed from HMRC by the business.

TAX POINT

You will note the date/TAX POINT on the invoice earlier in the chapter. The time of supply or TAX POINT is an important date as it is the date on which the transaction takes place for the purpose of deciding which VAT return/tax period the transaction should be included in.

When goods are supplied, the BASIC TAX POINT is the date of physical supply: the date on which the goods are taken away by the customer, sent to the customer or made available to the customer.

When services are provided, the basic tax point is the date on which the service is carried out and all work is finished.

The basic tax point is over-ridden if there is an ACTUAL TAX POINT.

An actual tax point is created if:

- The invoice is issued before the basic tax point, or
- Payment is received before the basic tax point.

Then the date of invoice or the payment is the actual tax point, depending upon which happens first.

If the date of physical supply is earlier than both the invoice date and the payment date, the basic tax point will still stand. However this can then be over-ridden if the invoice is issued within 14 days of the basic tax point. The invoice date will then become the actual tax point.

This 14-day rule may be varied provided that HMRC is contacted. For example an extension of the 14-day rule may be required if invoices are usually issued on a monthly basis.

If a VAT invoice is issued more than 14 days after the basic tax point without approval to extend the 14-day rule, the tax point reverts to the basic tax point, ie the date on which the goods or services were supplied.

HOW IT WORKS

To identify the relevant tax point of a transaction you need to go through the following steps:

Step 1   Identify the following three dates:

BASIC TAX POINT (date of physical supply)

Invoice date

Payment date

Step 2   Work out which of these is the earliest date.

Step 3   Follow the decision tree:

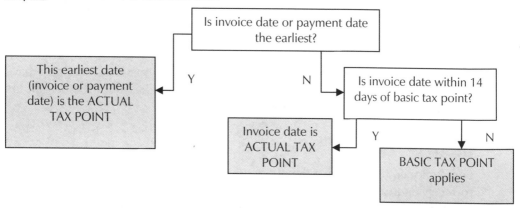

Importance of the tax point

The importance of the tax point, whether it is the basic tax point or the actual tax point, is that:

- The rate of VAT is fixed by the tax point, particularly important where there is a change in the rate of VAT; and

- The output tax must be paid over to HMRC by the supplier, and the input tax can be reclaimed by the purchaser, at the end of the period in which this tax point falls.

Task 4

A business sends goods out to a customer on 15 May 20X0. The VAT invoice is then sent later and is dated 20 May 20X0. The customer paid the invoice on 20 June 20X0. What is the tax point for these goods?

	✔
15 May 20X0	
20 May 20X0	
20 June 20X0	

Pro forma invoices

As we saw earlier, sometimes suppliers send out pro forma invoices. These have no relevance for tax point. The tax point is determined based on the date of the real VAT invoice, payment or supply.

Deposits

Sometimes customers pay a deposit in advance. This often happens as a response to receiving a pro forma invoice. If a deposit is paid, there will be separate tax points for the deposit and the balancing payment.

HOW IT WORKS

On 1 August a customer sent in a 15% deposit with an order. The goods were sent out to the customer on 6 August, and an invoice issued on 25 August. The customer paid the remaining 85% on 30 September.

The tax point for the deposit is determined by looking at:

- The basic tax point (delivery date)   6 August
- The invoice date   25 August
- The deposit payment date   1 August

Actual tax point is created as deposit is paid before the basic tax point.

Tax point for the deposit is 1 August (actual tax point)

The tax point for payment of the balance is determined by looking at:

- The basic tax point (delivery date)   6 August
- The invoice date   25 August
- The date of payment of the balance   30 September

The basic tax point is the earliest date so no actual tax point is created. Also the invoice date is more than 14 days after the basic tax point, so invoice date can be ignored.

Tax point for the balance is 6 August (basic tax point)

Task 5

A business received an order with a 10% deposit from a customer on 2 June 20X0. The goods were sent out to the customer on 11 June 20X0. The VAT invoice for the full amount is dated 29 June 20X0. The customer paid the remaining 90% on 31 July 20X0. Identify ONE or TWO tax point(s) for these goods.

	✓
2 June 20X0	
11 June 20X0	
29 June 20X0	
31 July 20X0	

THE VAT ACCOUNT

The central record that is used to record the overall VAT position and complete the VAT return, is the VAT ACCOUNT, or as it is sometimes referred to in a business's ledger, the VAT CONTROL ACCOUNT. Here all of the entries from the accounting records such as the sales and purchases day books are entered and the amount of tax due to, or reclaimable from HMRC is calculated for the period.

Note that the format of the VAT account we use here may look slightly different to the double-entry accounts you are used to. In particular, credit notes received are deducted from input tax and credit notes issued are deducted from output tax ie we include negative entries. This format allows us to use it as a central account to collect data for the VAT return. We will build up this account as we work through the Text bringing together the data required to complete a VAT return.

HOW IT WORKS

Given below is a typical VAT account set out in the manner suggested by HMRC in The VAT Guide, however any form of account which contains the same information would be acceptable.

VAT ACCOUNT

VAT deductible – input tax	£	VAT payable – output tax	£
VAT on purchases – from the purchases day book	4,090.17	VAT on sales – from the sales day book	6,135.65
VAT on purchases – from the cash payments book	670.54	VAT on sales – from the cash receipts book	1,010.90
Sub-total	4,760.71	**Sub-total**	7,146.55
Less:		Less:	
VAT on credit notes from suppliers – purchases returns day book	–56.80	VAT on credit notes to customers – sales returns day book	–79.77
Total tax deductible	4,703.91	**Total tax payable**	7,066.78
		Less: total tax deductible	–4,703.91
		Payable to HMRC	2,362.87

In later chapters we will return to the VAT account to add more entries.

VAT deductible – input tax

- The VAT on credit purchases is taken from the VAT column of the purchases day book and the VAT on cash purchases is taken from the VAT column of the cash payments book and petty cash payments book – these totals should be posted regularly from the day books to the VAT control account, usually on a weekly or a monthly basis

- The deduction for VAT on credit notes from suppliers is taken from the VAT column total of the purchases returns day book.

VAT payable – output tax

- The VAT on credit sales is taken from the VAT column of the sales day book and the VAT on cash sales is taken from the VAT column of the cash receipts book – these totals should be posted regularly from the day books to the VAT control account usually on a weekly or monthly basis

- The deduction for VAT on credit notes to customers is taken from the VAT column of the sales returns day book.

Tax payable

- The total tax deductible (input tax) is taken away from the total tax payable (output tax) to give a balance on the VAT account.

- If there is an excess of output VAT, tax is payable to HMRC for the period.

- If the total tax payable is less than the total tax deductible, there is an excess of input VAT, and tax is reclaimable/recoverable from HMRC for the period.

It is important to understand the balance on the VAT account should agree to the figure on the VAT return, which we will see later in this Text.

Much of the information covered in this chapter is available to view throughout the live assessment within the reference material. You should familiarise yourself with this document (included at the back of this Text) and practise using it when attempting any Tasks.

CHAPTER OVERVIEW

- A VAT-registered business making a supply to another VAT-registered business, must issue a valid VAT invoice within 30 days of making the supply

- If goods are supplied by a retailer for less than £250, including VAT, a less detailed VAT invoice can be issued which shows only the VAT inclusive amount and the rate of VAT – however if the customer asks for a full VAT invoice, this must be supplied

- If a pro forma invoice is sent out to a potential customer this must be clearly marked "This is not a VAT invoice" as the customer cannot use it to reclaim any input VAT

- The basic tax point is the date of physical supply. This basic tax point can be over-ridden by the actual tax point. The actual tax point can be created if an invoice is issued or a payment received before the goods or services are sent out, or by sending out an invoice after the supply of the goods providing that this is within 14 days of the supply

- The central accounting record for recording VAT is the VAT control account which lists all of the VAT deductible, or input tax, on the debit side and all of the VAT payable, output tax, on the credit side – the balance on this account is the amount of VAT due to or from HMRC for the period

Keywords

VAT invoice – an invoice that allows input VAT to be claimed or output VAT to be charged

Less detailed invoice – an invoice that can be issued by a retailer if the VAT-inclusive value of goods supplied is less than £250

Pro forma invoice – often used to offer goods to potential customers. It is not a valid VAT invoice

Tax point – the date which determines when the VAT must be accounted for to HMRC

Basic tax point – the date on which goods are delivered or services provided

Actual tax point – a further date that can over-ride the basic tax point if certain conditions are met

VAT account – the ledger account in which all amounts of input tax and output tax are recorded

TEST YOUR LEARNING

Test 1

Which TWO of the following statements about pro forma invoices are correct? Tick the relevant boxes below.

	✓
A pro forma invoice is always sent out when goods are sent to customers, before issuing the proper invoice	
A pro forma invoice should always include the words 'This is not a VAT invoice'	✓
A customer can reclaim VAT stated on a pro forma invoice	
A pro forma invoice is sent out to offer a customer the chance to purchase the goods detailed	✓

Test 2

In each of the following situations state the tax point and whether this is a basic tax point or an actual tax point (B or A):

	Date	Basic/ Actual
An invoice is sent out to a customer for goods on 22 June 20X0 and the goods are dispatched on 29 June 20X0	22	A
Goods are sent out to a customer on 18 June 20X0 and this is followed by an invoice on 23 June 20X0	23	A
A customer pays in full for goods on 27 June 20X0 and they are then delivered to the customer on 2 July 20X0.	27	A

Test 3

Given below is information about the VAT of a business that has been taken from the books of prime entry:

£

VAT figures

From the sales day book	9,147.96
From the sales returns day book	994.67
From the purchases day book	6,344.03
From the purchases returns day book	663.57
From the cash receipts book	1,662.78
From the cash payments book	936.58

You are to write up the VAT account.

VAT ACCOUNT

VAT deductible	£	VAT payable	£
PDB	6344·03	SDB	9147·46
CPB	936·58	cash receipt	1662-78
SRDB	994·67	Purchase return	663-57
Total VAT deductible		Total VAT payable	
	8275-28		11473-81

3198·53 payable

Picklist:

- Sales day book
- Sales returns day book
- Purchases day book
- Purchases returns day book
- Cash receipts book
- Cash payments book
- Less VAT deductible
- Less VAT payable
- Due to HMRC
- Reclaimed from HMRC

Test 4

Decide whether the following statements are true or false. Tick the relevant boxes below.

	True ✓	False ✓
If input VAT is greater than output VAT on the return, VAT is payable to HMRC		✓
If output VAT is greater than input VAT on the return, VAT is repayable from HMRC	✓	✓

chapter 3:
TYPES OF SUPPLY

── **chapter coverage** 📖 ──

The VAT treatment of a supply depends on whether VAT needs to be charged and, if so, at which rate. There are special rules that apply when goods and services enter and exit the UK. The topics covered are:

✍ Types of supply

✍ Taxable supplies

✍ Imports and exports, acquisitions and despatches

TYPES OF SUPPLY

Supplies of goods or services fall into one of three categories:

- Outside the scope of VAT
- Exempt supplies
- Taxable supplies

Outside the scope of VAT

SUPPLIES OUTSIDE THE SCOPE OF VAT have no effect for VAT.

These include paying wages or dividends.

Exempt supplies

EXEMPT SUPPLIES are supplies on which no VAT is charged at all, at any rate. You are not required to know which specific items are treated as exempt supplies for the assessment, but examples include:

- Post Office postal services
- Education
- Healthcare
- Insurance
- Betting and gambling

If a supplier only makes exempt supplies then he cannot register for VAT (see later in this Text) and so cannot reclaim the input VAT on any of his purchases and expenses. For example, an insurance company cannot reclaim the VAT on its expenses as its supplies (selling insurance) are exempt. So the cost to the insurance company of its purchases and expenses is the VAT inclusive amount.

TAXABLE SUPPLIES

There are three rates of VAT in the UK:

- Standard rate 20%
- Reduced rate 5%
- Zero rate 0%

A trader making taxable supplies can register for VAT. Once registered, the trader must therefore charge VAT on his supplies at the relevant rate, but as a result can reclaim input VAT on his purchases and expenses.

Standard-rated supplies

The vast majority of supplies of goods and services are STANDARD-RATED SUPPLIES. A supply should be treated as standard-rated, ie charged VAT at 20%, unless it specifically fits into one of the other categories.

Reduced-rated supplies

A reduced rate of VAT (5%) applies to certain supplies such as domestic fuel and power. Think of these supplies as standard-rated supplies (but special rules apply to allow 5% VAT to be charged on them).

Zero-rated supplies

ZERO-RATED SUPPLIES are supplies of goods and services which are technically taxable but the law states that the rate of VAT on these goods is 0%. The main reason for this is that these zero-rated supplies are normally essential items which, if they were taxed, would be an additional burden to the less well-off.

As with exempt supplies you are not required to know which specific items are treated as zero-rated but examples include:

- Young children's clothes and shoes
- Most food purchased in shops (but not in restaurants)
- Bus and train fares
- Books
- Newspapers and magazines

The effect on a business which makes zero-rated supplies is that although it charges output VAT at 0% on its sales it is allowed to VAT register and so can reclaim any input VAT on its purchases. Therefore a bus company charges no VAT on its fares but it is able to reclaim from HMRC any VAT on its purchases and expenses such as fuel and service costs. So the cost to the bus company of its purchases and expenses is the VAT exclusive amount.

The difference between exempt supplies and zero-rated supplies is that if a supplier makes only exempt supplies then he cannot reclaim the input VAT on any of his purchases and expenses.

Task 1

The following businesses have just paid telephone bills of £1,200 (£1,000 plus VAT of £200).

What is the net cost incurred by each business in relation to the telephone bills?

Business type	Type of supply made	Net cost £
Insurance company	Only exempt supplies	
Accountancy firm	Only standard rated supplies	
Bus company	Only zero rated supplies	

IMPORTS AND EXPORTS/ACQUISITIONS AND DESPATCHES

The treatment of VAT on purchases of goods from other countries, and sales to other countries depends upon whether the other country is within the European Union (EU) or outside it.

If goods are brought into the United Kingdom from a country that is not part of the EU, this is known as an IMPORT, whereas goods that are purchased from another country within the EU are known as ACQUISITIONS.

If goods are sold to a country outside the EU, this is known as an EXPORT and if goods are sold to a country within the EU, this is known as a DESPATCH.

We look at each situation in turn.

Imports

If goods are purchased from a country outside the EU the following treatment is required for VAT:

- The VAT is normally deemed to be at the same rate as on a supply of the same goods in the UK. This VAT is usually paid by the customer to HMRC as the goods enter the UK (ie at the docks or the airport)

- The VAT paid at the docks/airport is then reclaimed as input tax on the VAT return

The net effect is the same as buying from a UK supplier:

- Buying from a UK supplier, the customer pays the VAT to the supplier (as part of the invoice total), then reclaims the input VAT from HMRC on the VAT return

- Buying from outside the EU, the customer pays the VAT to HMRC at the port or airport, then reclaims the input VAT from HMRC on the VAT return

Acquisitions

If goods are purchased by a UK buyer from a VAT-registered business in another EU country, and the goods are sent to the UK, the EU supplier will not charge VAT (neither will HMRC at the ports/airports).

Instead, the UK purchaser must charge himself the VAT due on those goods on his VAT return. This VAT can be treated as input tax as well as being an amount of output tax due to HMRC.

Again the net effect is the same as above BUT no cash changes hands.

- Buying from a supplier in another EU country the customer 'pays' output tax to HMRC on the VAT return, then 'reclaims' the input VAT from HMRC on the same VAT return (net effect nil)

Exports

Goods exported to any country outside the EU are normally treated as zero-rated supplies provided that there is documentary evidence of the export and that this is obtained by the supplier within three months of the supply.

Despatches

If goods are sold to an EU customer there are two different scenarios:

- If the EU customer is a **VAT-registered business** in the EU country he will be charged VAT at the ZERO rate. To benefit from zero rating, he must provide his **EU VAT-registration number** (which is then shown on the invoice). Additionally the VAT registration numbers of both the supplier and customer must include the EU country code (for example GB).

- If the customer is **not EU VAT registered** (or his EU VAT registration number has not been given) then UK VAT is charged as if a normal UK sale (ie STANDARD rate in most cases).

Below we will show how these transactions can be recorded in the VAT account, and later in this Text see how they are entered onto the VAT return. Details can also be found within the reference material provided in the assessment.

Task 2

A UK trader sells goods to both registered and non-registered traders elsewhere in the EU. If these goods had been sold in the UK they would have been standard-rated. Which of the following is the correct treatment assuming all other conditions are fulfilled? Tick ONE box.

To registered traders	To non-registered traders	✓
Zero-rated	Zero-rated	
Standard-rated	Zero-rated	
Zero-rated	Standard-rated	
Standard-rated	Standard-rated	

Task 3

Joe acquires goods from a VAT registered supplier in another EU country. Tick the box that describes how Joe should deal with this acquisition for VAT.

	✓
No VAT is charged by the EU supplier therefore can be ignored by Joe on his VAT return	
Joe must pay output VAT to HMRC at the port/airport and can reclaim input VAT on the next return	
Joe must charge himself 'output VAT' and 'reclaim input' VAT on the same return	

HOW IT WORKS

The VAT account from Chapter 2 is shown again below. The additional items shown in italics are explained below.

VAT ACCOUNT

VAT deductible – input tax	£	VAT payable – output tax	£
VAT on purchases – from the purchases day book	4,090.17	VAT on sales – from the sales day book	6,135.65
VAT on purchases – from the cash payments book	670.54	VAT on sales – from the cash receipts book	1,010.90
	4,760.71		7,146.55
VAT allowable on EU acquisitions	242.16	*VAT due on EU acquisitions*	242.16
Sub-total	5,002.87	**Sub-total**	7,388.71
Less:		Less:	
VAT on credit notes from suppliers – purchases returns day book	–56.80	VAT on credit notes to customers – sales returns day book	–79.77
Total tax deductible	4,946.07	**Total tax payable**	7,308.94
		Less: total tax deductible	–4,946.07
		Payable to HMRC	2,362.87

VAT deductible and payable

The VAT on **acquisitions** from other European Union countries is shown as both input tax and output tax as the VAT must be charged on the acquisition but can also be deducted as allowable input tax

The **value** of the supply or acquisition of goods from other EU countries will need to be shown on the VAT return separately which we will see later in this Text.

Much of the information covered in this chapter is available to view throughout the live assessment within the reference material. You should familiarise yourself with this document (included at the back of this Text) and practise using it when attempting any Tasks.

CHAPTER OVERVIEW

- In the UK there are three rates of VAT – the standard rate of 20%, a reduced rate of 5% for certain supplies such as domestic fuel and power, and the zero rate. There are other goods and services which are entirely exempt from VAT

- There is no VAT charged on either zero-rated supplies or exempt supplies – however if a business makes exempt supplies it cannot reclaim the input tax on its purchases and expenses – if the supplies made by the business are zero-rated then input VAT can be reclaimed

- Goods imported from outside the EU are normally deemed to be charged at the same rate as goods in the UK

- The VAT on acquisitions of goods from other EU countries is treated as both output tax and input tax

- Exports of goods to another country outside the EU are normally treated as zero-rated supplies.

- Despatches of goods to other EU countries are usually zero-rated if the customer is VAT-registered, and has provided his VAT-registration number. Otherwise, they are treated as if they were normal UK sales.

Keywords

Supplies outside the scope of VAT – supplies which have no effect for VAT purposes (salaries and dividends)

Exempt supplies – supplies on which no VAT is charged

Standard-rated supplies – goods and services which are taxable at a rate of 20%

Zero-rated supplies – goods and services which are taxable but the rate of tax on them is 0%

Imports – goods purchased from a country outside the European Union

Exports – goods sold to a country outside the European Union

Acquisitions – goods purchased from another European Union country

Despatches – goods sold to another European Union country

TEST YOUR LEARNING

Test 1

Name the three categories of supplies of goods and services for VAT.

Test 2

Input numbers where indicated below.

The three rates of VAT in the UK are:

	%
	%
	%

Test 3

Identify whether the following statements are true or false.

	True ✓	False ✓
If a business supplies zero-rated services then the business is not able to reclaim the VAT on its purchases and expenses from HMRC.		
A business makes zero-rated supplies. The cost to the business of its purchases and expenses is the VAT exclusive amount.		

Test 4

A UK VAT-registered business is exporting goods which are standard-rated in the UK to an American business. Which ONE of the following statements is correct? Tick the relevant box.

	✓
The goods will be treated as standard-rated in the UK if the American business is VAT-registered	
The goods will be treated as standard-rated in the UK provided documentary evidence of the export is obtained within three months	
The goods will be treated as zero-rated in the UK if the American business is VAT-registered	
The goods will be treated as zero-rated in the UK provided documentary evidence of the export is obtained within three months	

chapter 4:
VAT REGISTRATION AND DEREGISTRATION

chapter coverage 📖

During the life of a business there may be times when the person making supplies may want to register for VAT or may be required to VAT register. Similarly, there could be situations where that person may want to deregister. The topics covered are:

✎ Registration for VAT

✎ VAT deregistration

REGISTRATION FOR VAT

A business must register for VAT if its taxable turnover exceeds the registration limit, which from 1 April 2011 is £73,000. There are two ways in which this limit must be tested.

The registration threshold and a summary of these two tests are outlined within the reference material provided in the assessment.

Historic turnover rule

If, at the end of a month the **taxable turnover** (the value of a business's taxable supplies) for the previous 12 months (or for the period since the start of trade, if that is shorter) has exceeded the registration limit, £73,000, then the business must register for VAT.

HOW IT WORKS

Jack started in business on 1 July 2011. His monthly VAT exclusive turnover is:

	£
Standard-rated supplies	7,000
Zero-rated supplies	1,850
Exempt supplies	600
TOTAL	9,450

1   Calculate the VAT exclusive taxable turnover for each month (standard plus zero-rated supplies). Exclude both sales of capital assets and exempt supplies.

Taxable turnover is £8,850 per month (£7,000 + £1,850)

2   Work out when the £73,000 registration limit is exceeded (if at all), up to a maximum of a 12 month period.

After 8 months (28 February 2012) cumulative turnover is £70,800, so the limit is not exceeded.

After 9 months (31 March 2012) cumulative turnover is £79,650 so the limit is exceeded.

Therefore in this case, Jack must register for VAT after 9 months.

Future turnover rule

If, at any time, the taxable turnover (before any VAT is added) is expected to exceed the registration limit within the next 30 days alone, then the business must register for VAT.

HOW IT WORKS

Orla has been in business for many years with VAT exclusive turnover of approximately £6,000 per month (£72,000 per annum). On 24 November 2011 Orla won a major contract which will immediately bring in additional income of approximately £67,500 per month.

Taxable turnover in the next 30 days is £73,500 (£6,000 + £67,500), which exceeds the threshold, therefore Orla must register for VAT.

A business must be extremely careful to ensure that if either its turnover for the last 12 months or its expected turnover within the next 30 days will exceed the registration limit then it must apply to register for VAT.

If a business does not apply to register, then it is liable to a penalty under the standardised penalty regime (see Chapter 8). In addition, if HMRC discovers in the future that the business should have been registered, but wasn't, the business

- may have to repay all output VAT that should have been charged if it had registered but
- will not be allowed to reclaim any input VAT.

These rules apply to suppliers of both standard-rated and zero-rated goods and services.

New and growing businesses that are not VAT registered are therefore recommended to monitor their cumulative turnover on a monthly basis.

Once registered for VAT you are known as a **registered person**.

Task 1

Amy started trading on 1 August 2010. Her monthly sales (excluding VAT) are:

	£
Standard-rated supplies	7,850
Zero-rated supplies	1,070
Exempt supplies	700
	9,620

By what date will Amy exceed the threshold for VAT?

Voluntary registration

If a business's taxable turnover is below the annual registration limit it is still possible for the business to register for VAT on a voluntary basis. Why might a business do this?

The main advantage of voluntary registration is the ability to recovery input tax.

In particular, if a business makes zero-rated supplies then it may be advantageous to register for VAT.

- output VAT at 0% (ie nil) has to be charged on its sales but
- it can reclaim the input VAT on its purchases and expenses.

Therefore the business is in a net cash repayment position.

Some businesses may want to VAT register to improve the image of the business. However the disadvantages include:

- the administrative burden of preparing regular VAT returns,

- the potential for incurring penalties, and

- loss of business from non-registered customers if prices increase by output tax

Task 2

Decide why a business making taxable supplies might choose to register for VAT voluntarily. Tick ONE box.

	✓
Preparation of VAT returns would be optional	
Customers would benefit by being able to claim back input VAT	
Business would benefit by being able to claim back input VAT	

Registration decision tree

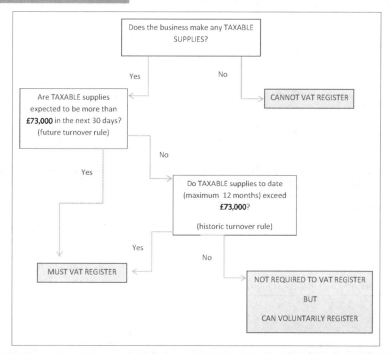

DEREGISTRATION

Voluntary deregistration

A VAT-registered business may find that its taxable turnover falls or is expected to fall. If the taxable turnover for the next 12 months is expected to fall beneath the deregistration limit, which from 1 April 2011 is £71,000, then the business can apply to HMRC to deregister.

Much of the information covered in this chapter is available to view throughout the live assessment within the reference material. You should familiarise yourself with this document (included at the back of this Text) and practise using it when attempting any Tasks.

CHAPTER OVERVIEW

- When a business's taxable turnover reaches the registration limit then the business must register for VAT, otherwise the business is liable to be fined

- Some businesses may find it advantageous to register for VAT although the registration limit has not been met – this is known as voluntary registration

- If a business's taxable turnover falls below the deregistration limit then the business can apply to HMRC to deregister

Keywords

Registration – the process required if a business making taxable supplies must, (if it exceeds the registration limits) or wants to, start charging (and recovering) VAT. VAT must be charged on taxable supplies from the date of registration

Deregistration – the process required to end a registration. VAT cannot be charged on any supplies from the date of deregistration

TEST YOUR LEARNING

Test 1

The following three businesses are trying to decide whether they need to register for VAT immediately or whether they just need to monitor the situation for the time being. Tick the correct box for each line.

		Register now	Monitor and register later
A	An existing business with total turnover for the previous 11 months of £70,000. Sales for the next month are unknown at present.		
B	A new business with an expected turnover for the next 12 months of £6,250 per month.		
C	An existing business with total turnover for the previous 12 months of £6,300 per month.		

Test 2

You have been contacted by a potential new client, Mrs Quirke. She has recently started trading as an interior designer. Complete the following letter to her explaining when her business must register for VAT.

AN Accountant
Number Street
London
SW11 8AB

Mrs Quirke
Alphabet Street
London
W12 6WM

Dear Mrs Quirke
VAT REGISTRATION

Further to our recent telephone conversation, set out below are the circumstances when you must register your business for VAT.

If the taxable turnover of your business at the end of a month, looking back no more than [   ] months, has exceeded the registration limit of £ [   ] then the business must apply to register for VAT.

Alternatively, if at any time, the taxable turnover (before any VAT is added) is expected to exceed the registration limit within the next [   ] then the business must apply to be registered for VAT. This would be the situation if, for example, you obtained a large one-off contract for, say, £75,000.

If you wish to discuss this in any more detail please do not hesitate to contact me.

Yours sincerely

AN Accountant

chapter 5:
OUTPUT TAX AND INPUT TAX

chapter coverage 📖

This chapter looks how to calculate the value of supplies and then at specific rules on the amount of output VAT charged, and the amount of input VAT which is recoverable. The topics covered are:

✍ Calculation of VAT

✍ Discounts

✍ Bad debt relief

✍ Cars, vans and fuel

✍ Business entertaining

✍ Partial exemption

CALCULATION OF VAT

VAT is charged on taxable supplies on the VAT exclusive or 'net' value. For standard-rated supplies the VAT is charged at 20%.

Sometimes the VAT-inclusive or 'gross' price is given, for example on less detailed or simplified VAT invoices. On such an invoice the actual amount of VAT charged is not shown separately. In order to calculate the amount of VAT included in this invoice, the VAT fraction of 20/120 or 1/6 (simplified) must be used on the gross amount.

Similarly you may need to calculate the VAT for reduced-rated supplies. The VAT fraction to be applied to VAT inclusive totals (gross amount) is 5/105 or 1/21 (simplified).

HOW IT WORKS

An invoice shows a total VAT-inclusive (gross) amount of £48.00. The amount of VAT at 20% included in this amount can be calculated as follows:

$£48.00 \times 20/120 = £8.00$

or

$£48.00 \times 1/6 = £8.00$

Another invoice for a reduced-rated supply shows a total VAT inclusive (gross) amount of £42.00. The VAT included in this amount can be calculated as

$£42.00 \times 5/105 = £2.00$

or

$£42.00 \times 1/21 = £2.00$

Task 1

Complete the following table.

Net	VAT rate	VAT	Gross
£	%	£	£
	20		52.20
	5		18.90

Rounding of VAT

VAT is calculated on the cost of the goods or services.

The total VAT on an invoice should be rounded down to the nearest 1p, and this is the treatment you should used when calculating VAT in the assessment.

The rules for rounding become more complex when applied to retailers, however these are not examinable in your assessment.

CASH OR SETTLEMENT DISCOUNTS

If a cash or settlement discount is offered to a customer, VAT is always calculated on the basis that the customer will take advantage of the discount. If the customer does not in fact take the settlement discount but pays the invoice in full there is no requirement to charge any additional VAT. The VAT that is charged and shown on the VAT invoice is the amount that should be accounted for on the VAT return.

HOW IT WORKS

Goods are supplied to a customer with a total VAT-exclusive list price of £800.00. The customer is allowed a 10% trade discount and is also offered an additional 3% settlement discount.

The VAT is calculated as follows:

	£
List price	800.00
Less: trade discount	80.00
Net price	720.00
Less: settlement discount	21.60
	698.40
VAT £698.40 × 20%	139.68
On the invoice you would see:	
VAT exclusive	720.00
VAT@20%	139.68
Invoice total	859.68

The customer could pay £859.68, or (£859.68 − £21.60) = £838.08 if the terms for receiving the cash discount are complied with. In either case, no adjustment is made to the amount of output tax.

Task 2

A business sells goods to a customer for £1,000. The customer is allowed a 20% trade discount and is offered a 2% settlement discount for payment within 14 days. If the goods are standard-rated how much VAT would be charged on them, assuming that the customer does not pay within the 14 day period?

	✓
£200.00	
£196.00	
£160.00	
£156.80	

BAD DEBT RELIEF

If goods or services are supplied on credit, the VAT will have been accounted for when the original VAT invoice was issued. If the debt is never paid by the customer and is written-off as irrecoverable or bad in the accounting records, BAD DEBT RELIEF is available. Bad debt relief means that it is possible to reclaim the VAT that will have been paid to HMRC on that supply, provided that certain conditions are met, most importantly that:

- The debt must be more than six months overdue (note this is measured from the date when the payment was due)
- The VAT must have been paid to HMRC
- The debt must be written-off in the business's accounts

The VAT on the irrecoverable or bad debt is shown on the VAT account as an INCREASE IN THE INPUT VAT to be reclaimed, NOT as a deduction from output tax.

HOW IT WORKS

An irrecoverable or bad debt arises, for example, when a customer has not paid after a long period of time or when a customer goes into liquidation.

Step 1   An entry is made into the journal to ensure that the irrecoverable or bad debt is reflected in the accounting records.

	Debit £	Credit £
Bad debts expense account (net amount)	192.00	
VAT account (INPUT VAT)	**38.40**	
Sales ledger control account (gross amount)		230.40

Step 2   When a period of more than six months since the due payment date has passed, bad debt relief can be claimed. THERE IS AN INCREASE IN INPUT VAT recoverable.

Task 3

What effect will claiming VAT bad debt relief have on the amount of VAT due to HMRC? Choose ONE answer.

	✓
The amount payable will increase	
The amount payable will decrease	

CARS AND VANS

Although we have said that VAT-registered businesses can reclaim VAT on purchases and expenses, there are some items of expenditure on which VAT cannot be reclaimed from HMRC.

When purchasing a car (eg company cars for sales people etc), including accessories fitted when purchased and delivery charges, VAT cannot be reclaimed. There are some exceptions to this for example if the car is used exclusively for business purposes (eg pool car), or used mainly as a taxi; for driving instruction; or for self-drive hire.

If VAT is not reclaimed on the original purchase price of a new car, the subsequent sale will be exempt for VAT purposes.

Note that VAT is generally recoverable on the purchase of a commercial vehicle such as a van.

VAT ON ROAD FUEL

Where a business purchases fuel for cars and retains a VAT invoice, it can reclaim the input VAT on that fuel, providing the fuel is only used for business. This input VAT will simply be part of the input VAT within the totals from the purchases day book or the cash book.

When there is private use of a car and fuel is provided, any of the following three arrangements can be put in place regarding the fuel.

- The input VAT can be apportioned to reflect the business: private use of the fuel,

- The FUEL SCALE CHARGE system can be used, with deduction of input VAT on the purchase of all fuel, or

- No input VAT reclaimed.

If no input VAT is reclaimed, this method must be applied to all vehicles including commercial vehicles.

With the fuel scale charge system, all of the input VAT can be reclaimed on the purchase of the fuel, then the appropriate fuel scale charge (based on the CO_2 emissions of the vehicle) is paid over to HMRC as output tax.

The fuel scale charge will increase the amount payable to HMRC.

HOW IT WORKS

An employee has a car provided by the business. The business purchases all petrol for the car and the employee uses the car for both business and private purposes.

Within the purchases day book or petty cash book are recorded VAT invoices for petrol. As a result, the input tax on these is reclaimed from HMRC each VAT period, as the VAT is included within the totals on those day books, ie the business is reclaiming VAT on all fuel including private fuel.

To offset against this claim for private fuel, the journal will include an entry for a fuel scale charge in relation to the private fuel used by the employee.

If, for example, the fuel scale charge for this vehicle is £28.83, the journal will include an entry

	Debit £	Credit £
Motor expenses account	28.83	
VAT account (OUTPUT VAT)		**28.83**

The OUTPUT VAT will increase.

HOW IT WORKS

The VAT account from earlier in the Text is shown again below. Additional items shown in italics are explained below.

VAT ACCOUNT

VAT deductible – input tax	£	VAT payable – output tax	£
VAT on purchases – from the purchases day book	4,090.17	VAT on sales – from the sales day book	6,135.65
VAT on purchases – from the cash payments book	670.54	VAT on sales – from the cash receipts book	1,010.90
	4,760.71		7,146.55
VAT allowable on EU acquisitions	242.16	VAT due on EU acquisitions	242.16
Bad debt relief	38.40	*Fuel scale charge*	28.83
Sub-total	5,041.27	**Sub-total**	7,417.54
Less:		Less:	
VAT on credit notes from suppliers – purchases returns day book	−56.80	VAT on credit notes to customers – sales returns day book	−79.77
Total tax deductible	4,984.47	**Total tax payable**	7,337.77
		Less: total tax deductible	−4,984.47
		Payable to HMRC	2,353.30

VAT deductible

- The bad debt relief is a claim for repayment of VAT already paid to HMRC on a sale to a customer who has never paid. The debt is over six months old and the irrecoverable (bad) debt has been written off in the accounting records. It is shown as INPUT VAT on the VAT return/ VAT account.

VAT payable

- The fuel scale charge is a payment corresponding to the element of private fuel consumption where VAT has been reclaimed on all fuel purchased by a business. It is shown as OUTPUT VAT on the VAT return/VAT account.

Note that the VAT account is building up as we progress through this Text. All entries that could appear within the account are being included for completeness. However a Task will not be set within the assessment that requires you to show the fuel scale charge within the VAT account.

BUSINESS ENTERTAINING

As mentioned above input VAT suffered on the purchase of a car cannot usually be reclaimed.

This is also the case for business entertaining. However, the input VAT on entertaining overseas customers and entertaining staff can be reclaimed.

Business entertaining includes free or subsidised entertainment or hospitality to anyone who is not an employee.

Usually the cost to a VAT-registered business of buying goods and services is the VAT-exclusive (net) amount. For example:

	£
Amount paid to supplier (VAT-inclusive)	1,200
Input VAT reclaimed from HMRC	(200)
Net cost to the business (VAT-exclusive)	1,000

However where VAT is irrecoverable (entertaining or cars) the cost to the business is the VAT-inclusive amount.

PARTIAL EXEMPTION

A taxable person may only recover the VAT on supplies made to him if it is attributable to his taxable supplies. Where a trader makes a mixture of taxable and exempt supplies (for example a dentist – dental services are exempt, but selling toothbrushes and toothpaste is taxable), he is classed as **partially exempt**. Where a trader is partially exempt, not all of his input VAT may be recoverable because some of it is attributable to his exempt supplies.

Attributing input tax

For a trader who is partially exempt, input VAT must be categorised between that relating to taxable supplies and that relating to exempt supplies.

Much of the input VAT may be directly attributable to either taxable supplies or exempt supplies. However a problem may arise when some of the input VAT relates to both types of supply, for example input VAT suffered on overheads. This unattributable VAT must be apportioned between the two types of supply. HMRC will agree various methods to do this. Once all the input VAT is attributed between the two types of supply the business will need to decide how much input VAT will be recoverable in total.

- **Attributable to making taxable supplies** (directly attributed eg toothbrushes in the example of a dentist plus the proportion of unattributed) – input tax is fully recoverable

- **Attributable to making exempt supplies** (directly attributed eg buying dentistry consumables in the dentist example plus the proportion of unattributed) – input tax not recoverable unless within certain limits

If the VAT incurred relating to EXEMPT supplies is then below a '**de minimis**' amount the VAT can be recovered in full.

Task 4

Decide whether each of the following statements is true or false.

	True ✓	False ✓
A registered business can reclaim all the input VAT attributed to zero-rated supplies.		
A registered business can reclaim all the input VAT attributed to standard rated supplies		
A registered business can reclaim all the input VAT attributed to exempt supplies		
A registered business can reclaim all the input VAT attributed to both taxable and exempt supplies providing certain de minimis tests are satisfied		

Much of the information covered in this chapter is available to view throughout the live assessment within the reference material. You should familiarise yourself with this document (included at the back of this Text) and practise using it when attempting any Tasks.

CHAPTER OVERVIEW

- VAT is charged on standard-rated supplies at 20%. Therefore, the VAT amount in a VAT-inclusive price is found by multiplying by 1/6

- VAT is charged on reduced-rate supplies at 5%. Therefore, the VAT amount in a VAT-inclusive price is found by multiplying by 1/21

- VAT is calculated on the cost of the goods or services after deduction of any trade discount. If a settlement discount is offered the VAT is calculated on the invoice amount less the discount – VAT is always rounded down to the nearest penny

- If a business writes-off a bad debt that is more than six months old and the output VAT on the supply has already been paid to HMRC, this VAT can be reclaimed from HMRC as input tax

- The VAT on business entertainment expenses of UK customers and the purchase of cars for use within a business is non-reclaimable

- If a VAT-registered business makes both taxable and exempt supplies the recovery of input tax will be restricted subject to the *de minimis* limits

Keywords

Bad debt relief – a reclaim of output VAT when a written off debt is more than six months overdue

Fuel scale charge – an output VAT charge to offset against the input VAT reclaimed on fuel purchased for private use

Partial exemption – when a business makes a mixture of taxable and exempt supplies then input VAT attributable to exempt supplies may only be reclaimed subject to satisfying de minimis tests

TEST YOUR LEARNING

Test 1

Business C sells goods to Business D for £384.00 plus the standard rate of VAT. Both businesses are VAT-registered.

(a)

The VAT is £	

(b) Which business will treat it as output tax and which will treat it as input tax?

	Output tax ✓	Input tax ✓
Business C		
Business D		

Test 2

Identify which two of the following types of expenditure have irrecoverable input tax

	✓
Staff party	
Car for sales manager	
Photocopier	
Entertaining UK clients	

Test 3

For each of the following situations calculate the amount of standard-rated VAT that would appear on the invoice:

	£
A VAT-exclusive list price of £356.75 will have VAT of	
A VAT-exclusive list price of £269.00 where a trade discount of 15 % is given will have VAT of	
A VAT-exclusive list price of £250.00 where a 2.5% settlement discount is offered will have VAT of	
A VAT-exclusive list price of £300.00 where a trade discount of 10% is given and a 3% settlement discount is offered, but not taken up will have VAT of	

Test 4

You have received four invoices from suppliers which show only the total VAT-inclusive price and the fact that all of the goods are standard-rated. For each invoice total determine the amount of VAT that is included.

Complete the following table.

VAT-inclusive £	VAT at 20 % £
42.88	
96.57	
28.20	
81.07	

Test 5

State three conditions for the VAT on an irrecoverable (bad) debt to be reclaimed from HMRC.

chapter 6:
VAT RETURN

chapter coverage 📖

So far we have considered the detailed rules for determining the correct amount of VAT. In this chapter we look at how this is reported to HMRC on the VAT return. The topics covered are:

✍ The VAT return

    – Completing the VAT return

    – Clearing the VAT account

✍ VAT and the effect on cash flow

✍ The VAT return online

THE VAT RETURN

A VAT RETURN, Form VAT 100, will normally need to be completed for each three-month accounting period, known as the tax period.

A business can apply to have a tax period that fits in with its financial year.

The VAT return is an extremely important area of the syllabus, it will account for half the marks in the assessment. Within section two there will always be a requirement to complete a VAT return extracting information from a set of accounts.

Completing the VAT return

The VAT return can be filed using a paper return or online using the HMRC website. If a paper return is filed, towards the end of each tax period a business will receive notice that a VAT return is due. The return must be completed and then submitted to the VAT Central Unit, arriving no later than the DUE DATE. For a paper return this is ONE MONTH after the end of the tax period.

Since 1 April 2010, all newly registered VAT traders (whatever their turnover) and all those with sales of £100,000 or more (excluding VAT), have been legally required to file their VAT returns online and pay electronically. For periods beginning on or after 1 April 2012, VAT-registered businesses with a VAT-exclusive turnover of less than £100,000 will also be required to file their returns online and pay electronically.

Businesses which file and pay VAT electronically automatically receive a seven-day extension to the usual due date. For example, a business which has a VAT quarter ending 31 March 2011 would normally have to submit its VAT return and pay the VAT due by 30 April 2011. Under electronic filing, this date moves to 7 May 2011.

The emphasis on differentiating between the paper and online return for the purpose of your assessment should only be placed on the difference in due dates, not on the difference in the format, or the way in which to fill them out. Although the online return (see later in this chapter) is very similar to the paper return, some of the boxes are completed automatically when using the online return. This will not be done for you in the assessment.

You will only be expected to know how to complete the format presented to you in the computer based assessment. Therefore we will complete the return as you would expect to see them in the assessment.

Information on due dates will be provided during the assessment within the reference material.

Boxes 1 to 9, the number entry boxes, of the VAT return are shown on the next page.

VAT due in this period on **sales** and other outputs (Box 1)

VAT due in this period on **acquisitions** from other **EC Member States** (Box 2)

Total VAT due (**the sum of boxes 1 and 2**) (Box 3)

VAT reclaimed in the period on **purchases** and other inputs, including acquisitions from the EC (Box 4)

Net VAT to be paid to HM Revenue & Customs or reclaimed by you (**Difference between boxes 3 and 4**) (Box 5)

Total value of **sales** and all other outputs excluding any VAT. **Include your box 8 figure** (Box 6)

Whole pounds only

Total value of purchases and all other inputs excluding any VAT. **Include your box 9 figure** (Box 7)

Whole pounds only

Total value of all **supplies** of goods and related costs, excluding any VAT, to other **EC Member States** (Box 8)

Whole pounds only

Total value of all **acquisitions** of goods and related costs, excluding any VAT, from other **EC Member States** (Box 9)

Whole pounds only

The boxes are completed as follows:

Box 1   The total of the output VAT on sales, less the VAT on any credit notes issued, together with any fuel scale charges and adjustments for earlier period errors – see later in this Text.

Box 2   The VAT due on any acquisitions from other European Union countries.

Box 3   The total of boxes 1 and 2.

Box 4   The total of the input VAT on purchases and expenses being reclaimed less the VAT on any credit notes received. This total also includes the VAT on any acquisitions from other EU countries, bad debt relief, and any adjustments for errors on previous VAT returns – see later in this Text.

Box 5   Deduct the figure in box 4 from the figure in box 3 and enter in box 5. If the figure in box 3 is larger than that in box 4, then this total is the amount due to HMRC. If the figure in box 3 is less than the figure in box 4, then the total is the amount that is due from HMRC.

Box 6   The total of all sales less credit notes. This total is excluding VAT but should include the net amount of sales that are standard-rated, zero-rated and exempt as well as any supplies to EU member countries.

Box 7   The total of all purchases and other expenses – less any credit notes. Again, this figure should be the total excluding any VAT and should include standard-rated, zero-rated and exempt supplies. This total should also include any acquisitions from EU member countries.

Box 8   Fill in box 8 with the total value, excluding VAT of all supplies of goods and related services to other EU member countries.

Box 9   Fill in box 9 with the total of all acquisitions of goods and related services, excluding VAT, from EU member countries. (Related services includes items such as freight costs and insurance for the goods.)

HOW IT WORKS

We will now use the VAT account from earlier in the Text to illustrate how to complete the VAT return for the period.

VAT ACCOUNT

VAT deductible – input tax	£	VAT payable – output tax	£
VAT on purchases – from the purchases day book	4,090.17	VAT on sales – from the sales day book	6,135.65
VAT on purchases – from the cash payments book		VAT on sales – from the cash receipts book	
(606.60+ 63.94)	670.54		1,010.90
	4,760.71		7,146.55
VAT allowable on EU acquisitions	242.16	VAT due on EU acquisitions	242.16
Bad debt relief	38.40	Fuel scale charge	28.83
Sub-total	5,041.27	**Sub-total**	7,417.54
Less:		Less:	
VAT on credit notes from suppliers – purchases returns day book	−56.80	VAT on credit notes to customers – sales returns day book	−79.77
Total tax deductible	4,984.47	**Total tax payable**	7,337.77
		Less: total tax deductible	−4,984.47
		Payable to HMRC	2,353.30

Not all of the information for the VAT return is found in the VAT account so the various day books will need to be consulted as well. These are given below.

Sales day book summary (all UK)-*

	Zero-rated sales £	Standard-rated sales £	VAT £	Total £
Jan 20XX	592.21	11,250.10	2,250.02	14,092.33
Feb 20XX	1,123.79	9,274.55	1,854.91	12,253.25
Mar 20XX	1,865.67	10,153.60	2,030.72	14,049.99
Total	3,581.67	30,678.25	6,135.65	40,395.57

Purchases day book summary

	Zero-rated purchases	UK purchases Standard-rated purchases	VAT on UK purchases	EU purchases	Total
	£	£	£	£	£
Jan 20XX	823.10	7,854.15	1,570.83	421.40	10,669.48
Feb 20XX	1,295.50	8,456.25	1,691.25	392.55	11,835.55
Mar 20XX	551.20	4,140.45	828.09	396.85	5,916.59
Total	2,669.80	20,450.85	4,090.17	1,210.80	28,421.62

Sales returns day book summary

	Zero-rated sales	Standard-rated sales	VAT	Total
	£	£	£	£
Jan 20XX	5.21	120.10	24.02	149.33
Feb 20XX	10.45	137.25	27.45	175.15
Mar 20XX	9.93	141.51	28.30	179.74
Total	25.59	398.86	79.77	504.22

Purchases returns day book summary (all UK)

	Zero-rated purchases	Standard-rated purchases	VAT	Total
	£	£	£	£
Jan 20XX	15.89	50.00	10.00	75.89
Feb 20XX	-	56.00	11.20	67.20
Mar 20XX	-	178.00	35.60	213.60
Total	15.89	284.00	56.80	356.69

Cash receipts book summary

	Net	VAT	Total
	£	£	£
Jan 20XX	1,234.40	246.88	1,481.28
Feb 20XX	1,867.31	373.46	2,240.77
Mar 20XX	1,952.80	390.56	2,343.36
Cash sales total	5,054.51	1,010.90	6,065.41

Cash payments book summary

	Net	VAT	Total
	£	£	£
Jan 20XX	824.45	164.89	989.34
Feb 20XX	956.76	191.35	1,148.11
Mar 20XX	1,251.80	250.36	1,502.16
Cash purchases	3,033.01	606.60	3,639.61

Petty cash payments book summary

	Net £	VAT £	Total £
Jan 20XX	121.21	24.24	145.45
Feb 20XX	98.15	19.63	117.78
Mar 20XX	100.36	20.07	120.43
Cash purchases	319.72	63.94	383.66

Journal (extract)

	Debit £	Credit £
Irrecoverable (bad) debt expense account	192.00	
VAT account	38.40	
Sales ledger control account		230.40
The write off of an irrecoverable (bad) debt (more than 6 months overdue)		
Motor expenses	28.83	
VAT account		28.83
Fuel scale charge for petrol on car provided for employee		

There were no sales to other countries but the value of the acquisitions from EU countries as shown in the purchases day book was £1,210.80 plus VAT.

The business also had an irrecoverable (bad) debt and provided petrol for business and private use for an employee's car. The details of these are shown in the extract from the journal above.

The business's name and address is Far Flung Creations, Zebra House, Horniman Street, Belsing, BE4 6TP. The VAT return is for the tax period ending 31 March 20XX and the business's VAT registration number is 382 6109 14.

How to complete the VAT return

The return is for the first period in 20XX ie to 31 March 20XX.

Now to complete the boxes. Note that figures are shown in pounds and pence in boxes one to five, with the TOTAL being rounded down to pounds for box 6.

WORKINGS:		£
Box 1	VAT on sales from the sales day book	6,135.65
	VAT on sales from the cash receipts book	1,010.90
	VAT on fuel scale charge	28.83
	Less: VAT on credit notes	(79.77)
		7,095.61
Box 2	VAT on EU acquisitions (1,210.80 x 20%)	242.16

Box 3	Total of box 1 and box 2 £7,095.61 + £242.16	7,337.77
Box 4	VAT on purchases from purchases day book	4,090.17
	VAT on purchases from cash payments book	606.60
	VAT on purchases from petty cash payments book	63.94
	VAT on EU acquisitions	242.16
	Bad debt relief	38.40
	Less: VAT on credit notes from suppliers	(56.80)
		4,984.47
Box 5	Net VAT due Box 3 minus box 4	
	£7,337.77-£4,984.47	2,353.30

Boxes 6 to 9 deal with sales and purchases before any VAT is added. Note that for these boxes no pence are needed.

Box 6	Zero-rated credit sales	3,581.67
	Standard-rated credit sales	30,678.25
	Cash sales	5,054.51
	Less: zero-rated credit notes	(25.59)
	standard-rated credit notes	(398.86)
		38,890
Box 7	Zero-rated credit purchases	2,669.80
	Standard-rated credit purchases	20,450.85
	Cash purchases	3,033.01
	Petty cash purchases	319.72
	EU acquisitions	1,210.80
	Less: zero-rated credit notes	(15.89)
	standard-rated credit notes	(284.00)
		27,384
Box 8	EU sales from sales day book	0
Box 9	EU acquisitions from purchases day book	1,210

THE RETURN

VAT due in this period on **sales** and other outputs (Box 1)

7,095.61

VAT due in this period on **acquisitions** from other **EC Member States** (Box 2)

242.16

Total VAT due (**the sum of boxes 1 and 2**) (Box 3)

7,337.77

VAT reclaimed in the period on **purchases** and other inputs, including acquisitions from the EC (Box 4)

4,984.47

Net VAT to be paid to HM Revenue & Customs or reclaimed by you (**Difference between boxes 3 and 4**) (Box 5)

2,353.30

Total value of **sales** and all other outputs excluding any VAT. **Include your box 8 figure** (Box 6)

38,890

Whole pounds only

Total value of purchases and all other inputs excluding any VAT. **Include your box 9 figure** (Box 7)

27,384

Whole pounds only

Total value of all **supplies** of goods and related costs, excluding any VAT, to other **EC Member States** (Box 8)

0

Whole pounds only

Total value of all **acquisitions** of goods and related costs, excluding any VAT, from other **EC Member States** (Box 9)

1,210

Whole pounds only

Note that if a paper return was being completed, HMRC would expect you to write 'none' if there is a box with no entry. However for the purpose of the assessment, you should insert a zero.

A paper return also has to be signed and dated, but again, you will not see this in the assessment. The return should then submitted to the VAT CENTRAL UNIT to be received no later than the due date. A copy should be kept for the businesses records.

Task 1

Identify which ONE of the following statements in relation to acquisition of goods from other EU countries and how they are dealt with on the VAT return is correct.

.	✓
Input tax paid at the ports is reclaimed as input tax on the VAT return	
They are shown as both input tax and output tax on VAT return	
They are zero rated and so do not feature on VAT return	
They are exempt and so do not feature on VAT return	

Clearing the VAT account

When the amount of tax due to HMRC is paid, then the double entry will be to credit the bank account and debit the VAT account, thereby clearing the account of any balance before the postings for the next period take place – this is illustrated below:

VAT ACCOUNT

VAT deductible – input tax	£	VAT payable – output tax	£
VAT on purchases – from the purchases day book	4,090.17	VAT on sales – from the sales day book	6,135.65
VAT on purchases – from the cash payments books		VAT on sales – from the cash receipts	
(606.60 + 63.94)	670.54	book	1,010.90
	4,760.71		7,146.55
VAT allowable on EU acquisitions	242.16	VAT due on EU acquisitions	242.16
Bad debt relief	38.40	Fuel scale charge	28.83
Sub-total	5,041.27	**Sub-total**	7,417.54
Less:		Less:	
VAT on credit notes from suppliers – purchases returns day book	−56.80	VAT on credit notes to customers – sales returns day book	−79.77
Total tax deductible	4,984.47	**Total tax payable**	7,337.77
		Less: total tax deductible	−4,984.47
Cash paid	2,353.30	**Payable to HMRC**	2,353.30

It is important to understand that the balance on the VAT account should agree to the figure on the VAT return.

Task 2

Identify which of the following statement(s) is/are correct. There may be more than one correct statement.

	✓
VAT charged at the fuel scale rate increases output VAT and is shown in Box 1	
VAT on EU acquisitions increases both input VAT and output VAT and is shown in box 1 & 4	
Credit notes received from suppliers reduce input VAT and are shown in box 4	
Credit notes issued to customers reduce output VAT and are shown in box 1	

VAT AND THE EFFECT ON CASH FLOW

The VAT payment must be submitted along with the VAT return by the DUE DATE.

With a paper return the payment can be sent by post and must be made no later than ONE MONTH after the end of the tax period. If, however, the payment is made electronically the taxpayer has an additional SEVEN calendar days to make the payment.

Where the VAT return is submitted online, the taxpayer must pay electronically and therefore has an additional seven calendar days for the payment to reach HMRC. Where the return is submitted online and the VAT paid by direct debit, it will usually be collected a further three days after the additional seven days.

These payment deadlines can be viewed throughout the assessment within the reference material.

VAT can be a substantial payment for a business to make. Provision should therefore be made to ensure that cash is reserved to pay the VAT after each period.

The person responsible for preparing the VAT return must set timescales for information to be provided to them on a timely basis and to ensure that they have sufficient time to prepare the return before the deadline. Once the return details have been finalised, they must contact the person responsible for paying the VAT to ensure that payment is made by the due date.

Within a communication task in the assessment, you may be asked to communicate payment information including amounts and time limits to a colleague within your organisation, or to a client. This may be by email.

Task 3

Using the details from the example above complete the email below.

To: Finance Director
From: Accounting Technician
Date: 25 April 20XX
Subject: VAT return to 31 March 20XX

Please be advised that I have now completed the VAT return for the quarter to 31 March 20XX. If you are in agreement with the figures shown in the return please could you arrange an electronic payment of

£ [＿＿＿＿＿＿＿＿] (number)

to be made by [＿＿＿＿＿＿＿＿] (date)

If you wish to discuss this further please feel free to call me.

Kind regards

THE VAT RETURN ONLINE

The online VAT return is very similar in appearance to the paper return. However, some of the boxes are completed automatically, for example box 3 is completed automatically, as the addition of boxes 1 and 2.

Once the relevant boxes have been completed there is the opportunity to review the return prior to pressing the 'submit' button. It is also possible to save a partially complete return which is useful if you need to get someone to review the actual return before you press 'submit'. Pressing 'submit' has the same effect as signing the declaration at the bottom of the paper return.

Once submitted the taxpayer is able to print a copy of the return and to obtain a submission reference number. Completed VAT returns for your business will be viewable by you on the HMRC website for 15 months.

A copy of the online return is shown below for completeness, however as mentioned above the key is to ensure that you are familiar with the version that you will see in the assessment.

Submit a return

VAT period
Period: 03 11
Date from:
01 Jan 2011
Date to:
31 Mar 2011
Due date:
07 May 2011 ⑦

Business details
VAT Registration Number:
382 6109 14
Business name:
FAR FLUNG CREATIONS
Business address:
ZEBRA HOUSE
HORNIMAN STREET
BELSING
BE4 6TP

Enter VAT return figures ⑦

Please enter the information in the boxes below and click 'Next' to proceed.

* indicates required information

Please note: Enter values in pounds sterling, including pence, for example 1000.00.

Important note

Your 'Total VAT due (Box 3)' and 'Net VAT to be paid to HM Revenue & Customs or reclaimed by you (Box 5)' figures will be calculated automatically when you click 'Next'. The figures will then be displayed on the next screen.

Before entering the figures please follow the link Filling in your VAT Return (opens in a new window)

VAT due in this period on **sales** and other outputs (Box 1):   [   ] ⑦

VAT due in this period on **acquisitions** from other **EC Member States** (Box 2):   [   ] ⑦

Total VAT due **(the sum of boxes 1 and 2)** (Box 3):   **Calculated value**

VAT reclaimed in this period on **purchases** and other inputs, (including acquisitions from the EC)

(Box 4):*[   ] ⑦

Net VAT to be paid to HM Revenue & Customs or reclaimed by you **(Difference between boxes 3 and 4)** (Box 5):   **Calculated value**

Total value of **sales** and all other outputs excluding any VAT. **Include your box 8 figure** (Box 6):
[   ] ⑦

Whole pounds only
(If you use the Flat Rate scheme, in this box please enter the amount **including** VAT, not **excluding** VAT. See Public Notice 733 (opens in a new window) for further information).

Total value of **purchases** and all other inputs excluding any VAT. **Include your box 9 figure** (Box 7):
[   ] ⑦

Whole pounds only
Total value of all **supplies** of goods and related costs, excluding any VAT, to other **EC Member States**

(Box 8)   :*[   ] ⑦
Whole pounds only
Total value of all **acquisitions** of goods and related costs, excluding any VAT, from other **EC Member**

States (Box 9):   *[   ] ⑦
Whole pounds only

[Next] [Back]

Much of the information covered in this chapter is available to view throughout the live assessment within the reference material. You should familiarise yourself with this document (included at the back of this Text) and practise using it when attempting any Tasks.

CHAPTER OVERVIEW

- Normally every quarter the VAT return, Form VAT 100, must be completed and submitted to HMRC together with any payment by the due date.

- For a paper return this is one month after the end of the tax period

- Returns submitted online and payments made electronically have a 7 day extension to these deadlines

- The first five boxes of the VAT return can be completed from the figures in the VAT account

- Boxes 6 to 9 must be completed from the other accounting records of the business showing sales and purchases, despatches and acquisitions excluding VAT

Keywords

VAT return – Form VAT 100 which must be completed to show the amount of VAT due or to be reclaimed, usually for the quarter

VAT Central Unit – the central VAT office that sends out the VAT returns and to whom the completed VAT return and any payment due must be sent

TEST YOUR LEARNING

Test 1

Given below are extracts from the books of prime entry for the business: Martin Trading, Blackness House, Jude Street, Clinford, CL3 6GH. The business's VAT registration number is 225 3756 12 and the tax period is March to June 20X1.

Sales day book summary

	Zero-rated sales £	Standard-rated sales £	VAT £	Total £
Total	13,447.67	45,267.40	9,053.48	67,768.55

Purchases day book summary

	Zero-rated purchases £	Standard-rated purchases £	VAT £	Total £
Total	7,447.30	30,627.55	6,125.51	44,200.36

Sales returns day book summary

	Zero-rated sales £	Standard- rated sales £	VAT £	Total £
Total	225.83	773.56	154.71	1,154.10

Purchases returns day book summary

	Zero-rated purchases £	Standard-rated purchases £	VAT £	Total £
Total	215.61	714.20	142.84	1,072.65

Cash receipts book summary

	Net £	VAT £	Total £
Cash sales	5,054.60	1,010.92	6,065.52

Cash payments book summary

	Net £	VAT £	Total £
Cash purchases	3,352.75	670.55	4,023.30

As well as the purchases shown in the purchases day book there were also acquisitions from EU countries totalling £2,256.07 plus £451.21 of VAT.

You are required to complete boxes 1 to 9 of the VAT return given.

VAT due in this period on **sales** and other outputs (Box 1)

VAT due in this period on **acquisitions** from other **EC Member States** (Box 2)

Total VAT due **(the sum of boxes 1 and 2)** (Box 3)

VAT reclaimed in the period on **purchases** and other inputs, including acquisitions from the EC (Box 4)

Net VAT to be paid to HM Revenue & Customs or reclaimed by you **(Difference between boxes 3 and 4)** (Box 5)

Total value of **sales** and all other outputs excluding any VAT. **Include your box 8 figure** (Box 6)

Whole pounds only

Total value of purchases and all other inputs excluding any VAT. **Include your box 9 figure** (Box 7)

Whole pounds only

Total value of all **supplies** of goods and related costs, excluding any VAT, to other **EC Member States** (Box 8)

Whole pounds only

Total value of all **acquisitions** of goods and related costs, excluding any VAT, from other **EC Member States** (Box 9)

Whole pounds only

Test 2

A business is filing its return for quarter ended 31 May 20X0. Fill in the table below outlining the correct dates for submission of VAT returns and payment of VAT

Return	Date	Payment	Date
Paper return		Cheque	
Online return		BACs	
Online return		Direct debit	

Dates to choose from:

30 June 20X0

7 July 20X0

10 July 20X0

chapter 7:
SCHEMES FOR SMALL BUSINESSES

---

chapter coverage 📖

Over many years it has been recognised that VAT has become a burden that is especially tough for small businesses. Several schemes have been devised in order to help small businesses. The topics covered are:

✍ Annual accounting

✍ Cash accounting

✍ Flat rate scheme

SPECIAL SCHEMES

There are a number of special schemes which make VAT accounting easier for small businesses.

Annual accounting scheme

The ANNUAL ACCOUNTING SCHEME is helpful to small businesses as it cuts down the administrative burden of VAT by allowing the business to submit one VAT return every 12 months. The VAT return is due within two months of the end of the year.

Note there is NO seven day extension to this deadline if submitted online.

Under this scheme the business makes nine (usually) equal monthly direct debit payments of 1/10 of the estimated amount of VAT liability for the year. If the business has been trading for a period of time, the estimate will usually be the liability of the previous 12 months. The first monthly payment is due at the end of month four, working through to the end of month 12.

The balancing payment will be due with the VAT return, within two months after the year end.

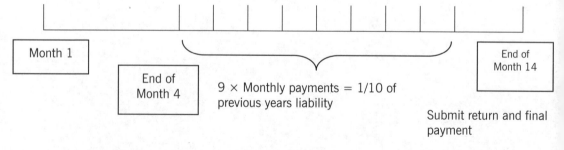

Use of this annual accounting scheme is a great help to a small trader as it means that he does not have to prepare a quarterly VAT return. However, it does mean that he must still keep accurate accounting records of the VAT information for a whole year.

The limits for joining and leaving this scheme are:

	VAT exclusive taxable turnover £
Join the scheme if turnover in the next 12 months is expected to be below (exclude capital supplies)	1,350,000
Leave the scheme if turnover in the previous 12 months exceeds	1,600,000

The advantages of the annual accounting scheme include:

- Only one VAT return each year instead of four
- Two months instead of one to complete and send the return and payment
- Ability to manage cash flow more accurately paying fixed amounts in each instalment
- Avoids the need for quarterly calculations for input tax recovery
- Can join the scheme immediately from date of registration

The disadvantages of the annual accounting scheme include:

- The need to monitor future taxable supplies to ensure turnover limit not exceeded
- Timing of payments have less correlation to turnover (and hence cash received) by the business
- Payments based on previous year's turnover may not reflect current year turnover which may be a problem if the scale of activities has reduced
- If regularly reclaim VAT, will only get one repayment per year

Task 1

A trader has joined the annual accounting scheme for the year ended 31 December 2012. Identify whether the following statement is true or false. (Insert a tick)

	True	False
The first payment due to HMRC is by 1 April 2012.		

Cash accounting scheme

Provided a business has a clean record with HMRC, it may be able to apply to use the CASH ACCOUNTING SCHEME. All VAT returns and payments must be up-to-date and the business must not have been convicted of a VAT offence or penalty in the previous 12 months.

The scheme allows the accounting for VAT to be based upon the date of receipt or payment of money rather than the tax point on an invoice.

This means the scheme gives automatic relief from irrecoverable (bad) debts since no output VAT is payable to HMRC if the customer does not pay.

The scheme is also very useful for a business which gives its customers a long period of credit or they are slow to pay, as it will not have to pay output tax until it is received.

Therefore OUTPUT VAT will be paid to HMRC later than if the business used the standard VAT accounting rules.

This may also apply if the business pays its suppliers promptly, with INPUT VAT being reclaimed at the same time or earlier than with standard rules.

The scheme would therefore be less beneficial for a business which receives a long period of credit from its suppliers, or is slow to pay, as they would not be able to reclaim the input tax until they have paid their suppliers. And if the business receives payment promptly from its customers, they may end up paying output tax earlier than with the standard rules.

VAT return and payment dates are as for the standard scheme, unless the business is also in the annual accounting scheme.

The limits for joining and leaving this scheme are:

	VAT exclusive taxable turnover £
Join the scheme if turnover in the next 12 months is expected to be below (exclude capital supplies)	1,350,000
Leave the scheme if turnover in the previous 12 months exceeds	1,600,000

Task 2

Would the cash accounting scheme improve the cash flow of a retail business that receives most of its sales in cash and buys most of its purchases on credit? Tick ONE of the boxes.

	✓
Yes, because they would be able to reclaim input VAT earlier	
Yes, because they would pay output VAT later	
No, because they would reclaim input VAT later	
No, because they would pay output VAT earlier	

Flat rate scheme

The FLAT RATE SCHEME allows a business to simplify its VAT accounting by calculating the VAT payment due as a percentage of its total VAT-inclusive turnover for the period. The business cannot however then reclaim VAT on purchases.

Businesses using the scheme would still need to issue VAT invoices to their VAT-registered customers, but do not have to record all the details of invoices issued or purchase invoices received to calculate VAT due.

HMRC set different flat rate percentages for different trade sectors ranging from 4% to 14.5%. This percentage is applied to the **VAT-inclusive** turnover of the business, which includes all zero rate and exempt income along with the standard rate income.

The main advantages of this scheme are:

- It simplifies the administration considerably, as VAT does not have to be accounted for on each individual sales and purchase invoice

- There can be less VAT payable to HMRC than under the normal rules

- Cash flow can be managed more easily as there is always a certainty as to what percentage of turnover will be paid to HMRC

- A discount is given in the first year of VAT registration of 1% reduction to the flat rate

The main disadvantages of this scheme are:

- VAT cannot be reclaimed on purchases and expenses

- The flat rate percentage is applied to all turnover including zero-rated and exempt supplies

This may result in more VAT payable than under standard VAT accounting rules, and so might not be suitable for the following type of businesses:

- Those in a trade with a high flat rate percentage

- Those making a lot of zero or exempt supplies

- Those who regularly receive a VAT repayment under standard VAT accounting

- Those whose purchases and expenses are mainly standard-rated

The limits for joining and leaving this scheme are:

	Turnover £
Join the scheme if VAT-exclusive TAXABLE turnover (excluding capital supplies) does not exceed	150,000
Leave the scheme if TOTAL value of VAT inclusive turnover (excluding capital supplies) exceeds	230,000

VAT returns and payments are made at the same time as for the standard scheme.

Task 3

A trader, making standard-rated (20%) supplies, has joined the flat rate scheme.

The flat rate percentage applying to his business sector is 8.5%.

His VAT exclusive turnover for the quarter is £30,000.

What is the VAT due to HMRC for the quarter?

	✓
£2,550	
£3,060	

Note that details on all three of these schemes are available to view throughout the live assessment within the reference material provided.

You should familiarise yourself with this document (included at the back of this Text) and practise using it when attempting any Tasks.

CHAPTER OVERVIEW

- If a VAT-registered trader has a turnover of less than £1,350,000 excluding VAT, then he may be eligible for the annual accounting scheme – under which nine monthly direct debit payments are made based upon an estimate of the VAT liability for the year. The tenth and balancing payment is made when the VAT return for the year is submitted within two months of the year end

- If a business has an annual turnover of less than £1,350,000, excluding VAT, it may be eligible for the cash accounting scheme whereby VAT has to be accounted for to HMRC on the basis of cash payments received and made, rather than on the basis of the tax point on the invoice

- If a business has an annual turnover of less than £150,000, it can simplify its VAT records by calculating its VAT payment as a percentage of total turnover instead of accounting for input and output tax on each individual purchase and sales invoice

Keywords

Annual accounting scheme – a method of accounting for VAT which does not require quarterly returns and payments – instead nine monthly direct debit payments and an annual return accompanied by the final payment

Cash accounting scheme – a method of accounting for VAT which allows VAT to be dealt with according to the date of payment or receipt of cash rather than the tax point on the invoice

Flat rate scheme – enables businesses to calculate their VAT payment as a percentage of total VAT-inclusive turnover

TEST YOUR LEARNING

Test 1

Complete the following letter to Jacob Lymstock, a client of yours who has a small business.

AN accountant
Number Street
London
SW11 8AB

Mr Lymstock
Alphabet Street
London
W12 6WM

Dear Mr Lymstock
ANNUAL ACCOUNTING SCHEME

I have recently been reviewing your files. I would like to make you aware of a scheme that you could use for VAT.

As the annual value of your taxable supplies, **(including/ excluding)** VAT and supplies of capital items, in the following 12 months is expected to be **(above/ below) £(1,350,000/1,600,000)** you can join the annual accounting scheme.

Under this scheme you make ▢ **(insert number)** monthly direct debit payments based upon an estimate of the amount of VAT due. The first of these payments is due at the end of the ▢ month of the accounting period. You must then prepare a VAT return for the year and submit it with the balancing payment, by **(30 days/ one month/ two months)** after the year end.

Use of this annual accounting scheme is a great help as it means that you only have to prepare ▢ **(insert number)** VAT return(s) each year.

If you wish to discuss this with me in more detail please do not hesitate to contact me.

Your sincerely

AN Accountant

Test 2

Complete the following statement.

If the annual value of taxable supplies, **(including/excluding)** VAT, is **(more/less)** than £**(1,350,000/1,600,000)** and provided that a trader has a clean record with HMRC, he may be able to apply to use the cash accounting scheme.

The scheme allows the accounting for VAT to be based upon the date of **(receipt and payment of money/invoice)**. This is particularly useful for a business which gives its customers a **(short/long)** period of credit whilst paying its suppliers promptly.

The scheme also gives automatic relief from ⬚⬚⬚⬚⬚⬚ so if the customer does not pay the amount due, then the VAT need not be accounted for to HMRC.

Test 3

An existing trader makes standard rated supplies and uses the flat rate scheme. The flat rate percentage that he must use is 11.5%.

For quarter ended 31 Mar 20X0 the trader had total turnover of £9,500 excluding VAT. He also had VAT-exclusive purchases of £3,000.

(a)   Which figure reflects the amount of VAT payable to HMRC?

	✓
£897.00	
£1,092.50	
£1,311.00	✔

(b)   In this quarter, would the trader have more or less VAT to pay to HMRC if he was not in the flat rate scheme.

	✓
More VAT is payable not using the flat rate scheme	
More VAT is payable using the flat rate scheme	

chapter 8:
ERRORS AND PENALTIES

chapter coverage 📖

The penalties and interest due when VAT requirements are not met are stringently applied. This is one of the reasons why many businesses who do not have to VAT register, choose not to do so. The topics covered are:

✍ Dealing with errors

✍ Penalties

ERRORS

A business may discover it has made an error or errors on a VAT return which it has already submitted.

If this is the case, the business will need to calculate the 'net' value of all errors found relating to returns that have already been submitted. The net error is any under-declaration of VAT less any over-declaration of VAT.

Any deliberate errors should not be included as they must be disclosed separately. They must be reported to the relevant HMRC VAT Error Correction Team, in writing and preferably using Form VAT 652 "Notification of Errors in VAT Returns".

Errors exceeding the error correction reporting threshold

If the net error was not deliberate, but is more than the greater of:

- £10,000 or

- 1% of turnover as per box 6 of the relevant return (subject to an overall £50,000 limit),

it will exceed the error correction reporting threshold and cannot be adjusted for on the next VAT return.

Instead the relevant HMRC VAT Error Correction Team must be informed in the same way as disclosing deliberate errors above.

Task 1

A business has turnover of £6.5 million. The output tax on its last VAT return was understated by £52,000. Tick ONE statement below.

	✓
A correction can be made on the next VAT return as the error is less than 1% of turnover	
A correction cannot be made on the next return as the error exceeds £10,000	
A correction cannot be made on the next return as the error exceeds £50,000	

Errors below the error correction reporting threshold

If the 'net' error is below the ERROR CORRECTION REPORTING THRESHOLD, corrections can be made on the next return.

For example, an understatement of output VAT on a previous return can be shown as an increase in the output tax on box 1 of the current return. Similarly an overstatement of input VAT on a previous return can be shown as a decrease in the input tax on box 4 of the current return.

The VAT account must show the value of the adjustment made on the return (see below).

Where more than one error has been made a single adjustment is made being the total of all errors made in the previous return.

If the net effect of all the errors is that input VAT was overstated on a previous return then the amount to be included as input tax on box 4 of the current return should be reduced accordingly.

If the net effect of all the errors is that output VAT was overstated on a previous return then the amount to be included as output tax on box 1 of the current return should be reduced accordingly.

In addition, the relevant HMRC VAT Error Correction Team may be informed, in writing and preferably using Form VAT 652. The relevant box on the form should be ticked to show that the error has been adjusted for on the return.

Task 2

A business made a 'small' overstatement of input tax on a previous return. What effect will this have on the current VAT payable to HMRC?

	✓
An increase in the VAT payable via the current return	
A decrease in the VAT payable via the current return	
No impact on the current return. It must just be separately declared	

HOW IT WORKS

The VAT account from earlier in the Text is shown again below. The adjustments for errors are shown in italics and are explained below.

VAT ACCOUNT

VAT deductible – input tax	£	VAT payable – output tax	£
VAT on purchases – from the purchases day book	4,090.17	VAT on sales – from the sales day book	6,135.65
VAT on purchases – from the cash payments book	670.54	VAT on sales – from the cash receipts book	1,010.90
	4,760.71		7,146.55
VAT allowable on EU acquisitions	242.16	VAT due on EU acquisitions	242.16
Net overclaim of input tax from previous returns	*–104.56*	*Net understatement of output tax on previous returns*	*287.52*
Bad debt relief	38.40	Fuel scale charge	28.83
Sub-total	4,936.71	**Sub-total**	7,705.86
Less:		Less:	
VAT on credit notes from suppliers – purchases returns day book	–56.80	VAT on credit notes to customers – sales returns day book	–79.77
Total tax deductible	4,879.91	**Total tax payable**	7,625.29
		Less: total tax deductible	–4,879.91
		Payable to HMRC	2,745.38

VAT deductible

- If there is a net over-claim of input tax from previous VAT returns it can be adjusted for in this VAT return provided that the net value of the errors does not exceed the error correction reporting threshold.

- Such errors relating to input VAT are included in box 4 of the VAT return, along with the usual total of input VAT being reclaimed.

VAT payable

- Alternatively if there is a net understatement of output tax from previous periods, it can be adjusted for in this VAT return provided that the net value of the errors does not exceed the error correction reporting threshold.

- Such errors relating to output VAT are included in box 1 of the VAT return, along with the usual total of output VAT payable.

Task 3

A business has made a small understatement of output tax in a previous quarter. Should this adjustment be shown on the latest VAT return, and if so where on the return?

	✓
No – not shown on the return	
Yes – shown in box 1	
Yes – shown in box 4	

PENALTIES

Penalties for careless and deliberate errors

Careless and deliberate errors will be liable to a penalty, whether they are adjusted on the VAT return or reported separately.

Where errors are made in VAT returns resulting in

- An understatement of the VAT liability, or
- A false or increased repayment of VAT

the penalty applied is likely to be the civil penalty of 'penalty for errors'.

If an error is neither careless (not taken reasonable care in making the return) nor deliberate, HMRC will expect steps to be taken to correct it, otherwise the error will be treated as careless and a penalty will arise.

Late VAT return or VAT payment

If a business does not submit a VAT return and pay over any VAT due by the due date, then that trader is in default and a SURCHARGE LIABILITY NOTICE will be served. The notice specifies a surcharge period of 12 months. If there is default involving the late payment of VAT (as opposed to simply a late return) within the surcharge period, then a surcharge is levied. This is a percentage of the unpaid VAT.

If the business does not send in a VAT return, then the amount of VAT owed will be assessed and the surcharge will be based upon this assessment.

Assessments

A VAT-registered business is legally obliged to submit a VAT return and pay any VAT owing by the due date. If a return is not submitted HMRC can raise an assessment based on what it believes is owed. If the business fails to notify HMRC within 30 days that the amount owing is actually greater than the amount assessed, the business may be liable to a penalty.

Failure to register for VAT

A penalty can be raised under the standardised penalty regime, for failure to notify HMRC of the liability to register by the proper date.

Failure to keep and retain records

As mentioned earlier in this Text, records should be retained for six years for VAT purposes, unless an agreement is reached with HMRC to dispose of them earlier. Where records have not been retained for this period, a penalty could be imposed.

Fraudulent evasion of VAT

Tax evasion consists of seeking to pay too little tax by deliberately misleading HMRC by suppressing information or providing it with false information. Tax evasion is illegal, as opposed to tax avoidance, which is more difficult to define, but broadly speaking is any legal method of reducing your tax burden.

Evasion of VAT includes falsely:

- Reclaiming input tax/understating output tax
- Obtaining bad debt relief
- Obtaining a repayment

Tax evasion is a criminal offence, but HMRC prefers to settle minor cases out of court with the payment of penalties and interest. HMRC will encourage cooperation and may reduce the penalty accordingly.

Extreme cases of tax evasion might result in fines and/or imprisonment.

Much of the information covered in this chapter is available to view throughout the live assessment within the reference material. You should familiarise yourself with this document (included at the back of this Text) and practise using it when attempting any Tasks.

CHAPTER OVERVIEW

- If a net error exceeding the error correction reporting threshold is discovered from a previous tax period, this cannot be adjusted in the VAT return. Instead voluntary disclosure should be made and the HMRC VAT Error Correction Team informed. A penalty might be imposed depending on the behaviour of the business.

- If a VAT return or payment is late, the taxpayer is served with a surcharge liability notice and may have a surcharge to pay if further payment defaults occur

- A number of other penalties apply for VAT purposes including failure to register and failure to keep records

- VAT evasion is a criminal offence and may give rise to fines and/or imprisonment

Keywords

Error correction reporting threshold – this is the threshold that dictates whether errors discovered on a previous return can be corrected on the next return or reported separately

Surcharge liability notice – this warns a business that its VAT return or payment was not received on time and if the business pays late within the next twelve months, a default surcharge will be due

Voluntary disclosure – the action of notifying HMRC of any error found from previous returns

Evasion of VAT – falsely reclaiming input VAT/understating output tax, obtaining bad debt relief or obtaining a repayment

TEST YOUR LEARNING

Test 1

Identify which one of the following statements is correct.

	✓
If a net error of more than the lower of £10,000 and 1% of turnover (subject to an overall £5,000 limit) is discovered it must be disclosed on Form VAT 652	
If a net error of more than the greater of £10,000 and 1% of turnover (subject to an overall £5,000 limit) is discovered it must be disclosed on Form VAT 652.	
If a net error of more than the lower of £10,000 and 1% of turnover (subject to an overall £50,000 limit) is discovered it must be disclosed on Form VAT 652.	
If a net error of more than the greater of £10,000 and 1% of turnover (subject to an overall £50,000 limit) is discovered it must be disclosed on Form VAT 652.	

Test 2

Identify whether the following statement is true or false.

Tax avoidance is illegal and could lead to fines and/or imprisonment

True ✓	False ✓

Test 3

Given below is information about the VAT of a business taken from the books of prime entry:

From the sales day book	3,572.15
From the purchases day book	1,825.67
From the cash receipts book	994.67
From the cash payments book	514.37
EU acquisitions	236.57
Bad debt relief	105.37
Output VAT underpaid in a previous period	44.79
Input VAT not reclaimed in a previous period	25.47

You are to write up the VAT account.

VAT ACCOUNT

VAT deductible	£	VAT payable	£
Total VAT deductible		Total VAT payable	

Picklist:

Sales day book
Purchases day book
Cash receipts book
Cash payments book
EU acquisitions
Bad debt relief
Undercharge of output VAT
Underclaim of input VAT
Less VAT deductible
Less VAT payable
Due to HMRC
Reclaimed from HMRC

chapter 9:
CONTACT WITH CLIENTS AND HMRC

---

chapter coverage 📖

An important part of dealing with VAT for an accountant is to be able to communicate information to both HMRC and clients, and to act professionally at all times. The topics covered are:

✎ Changes in VAT legislation and the impact on systems, staff and customers

✎ Seeking guidance from HMRC

CHANGES IN VAT LEGISLATION

Changes in VAT legislation are usually notified by HMRC to traders via bulletins or notices. If a change affects a certain sector of businesses, then the relevant businesses will receive a paper or e-mail version of the notice.

There was a change in the standard rate of VAT from 17.5% to 20% on 4 January 2011. In accordance with the guidance issued by AAT, when calculating VAT you should always use a standard rate of 20% regardless of the date of transaction. For your assessment you simply need an awareness of how such changes can impact on businesses.

A change in the standard rate of VAT affects all VAT-registered businesses.

Impact on accounting systems and internal staff

A change in VAT legislation, such as a change in VAT rate, may require the accounting systems to be adjusted.

A change in the VAT rate will mean that from a certain date a different amount of VAT must be charged on certain supplies. In most situations this is fixed by the tax point. For example, when the standard rate of VAT changed from 17.5% to 20% on 4 January 2011, a standard-rated supply of £1,000 (excluding VAT) gave rise to an invoice total of £1,175 if the tax point was before 4 January 2011, but £1,200 if the tax point was on or after 4 January 2011.

The business still only receives £1,000 after paying over the output tax to HMRC.

Where a business has a computerised accounting system/tills this can give rise to problems. The systems will be set to calculate VAT at a set percentage for certain supplies. In these circumstances it is usual for the company that developed the software package to give instructions as to how the VAT rate can be changed on the system. A business's IT team should therefore be informed of the rate change to make sure that they implement these changes to the computer system.

If a manual system is in use, the trader simply needs to ensure that they are careful about applying the correct VAT rate for the tax point of each particular supply. Therefore, sales ledger and purchase ledger staff should be informed to ensure invoices reflect the correct rate of VAT, remembering the rate of VAT must be relevant to the tax point, and not necessarily the invoice date.

A change in legislation may affect the actual price at which sales are made (if there are changes to the output VAT charged). See 'impact on customers' below. This is the case if there is a change of rate, therefore the sales team and marketing team within a business should be informed of the change.

In the assessment you may be expected to draft an internal memo or email to advise relevant members of staff of a change to the rate of VAT.

Impact on customers

If customers are VAT-registered then they should also be aware of changes in legislation, especially with something as significant as a change in VAT rates.

However, where customers are not VAT-registered, for example in a retail business, notice should be given to customers about changes in rates. In a retail environment this would usually be via notices displayed around the store. A change in rate could impact on the charge to the customer. Using the earlier example, an item costing a customer £1,175 on 3 January 2011 would cost £1,200 on 4 January 2011 if the trader intends to keep the same VAT-exclusive charge. An alternative is for the trader to keep the same VAT-inclusive price so that there is no impact on his customers. However, for an increase in VAT rate, this will reduce the trader's overall turnover as a greater proportion of this price charged will have to be paid to HMRC as output VAT.

Task 1

Doug is a retailer and has been selling goods to the general public for £235 (VAT-inclusive) while the VAT rate was 17.5%. (VAT fraction 7/47). When the VAT rate changed to 20% he did not want to change the cost of these goods to his customers who are not VAT-registered.

Work out for Doug the VAT-exclusive amount of the goods sold both before and after the change in the VAT rate.

VAT-inclusive £	VAT rate	VAT-exclusive £
235.00	17.5%	
235.00	20%	

CONTACT WITH HMRC

HMRC usually expect taxpayers to find answers to any queries on their website as mentioned earlier in the Text. However there is also a VAT HELPLINE where advice can be given to registered persons on most VAT matters. The Helpline can also be used to obtain copies of VAT publications.

The telephone number of the VAT Helpline can be found on the HMRC website.

Whenever a registered person contacts HMRC in writing or by telephone they should always quote their name, address, telephone number and the VAT registration number of the business, and keep a note of the conversation and the call reference given.

It is advisable to get written confirmation from HMRC about issues on which doubt may arise as to the correct VAT treatment.

In assessments, you will typically be required to seek guidance from HMRC in writing on some aspect of the organisation's affairs. The area that you have to enquire about may be very simple or it may be more complicated or obscure. If it is a simple point, then the task may require a brief explanation of the point as well as seeking more detailed guidance from HMRC. If the point is more complex then you will only be required to ask for guidance in an intelligent and professional manner, not to understand the sometimes complex provisions of VAT law.

Control visits from HMRC

From time to time an HMRC officer will visit a VAT-registered business (a control visit) in order to examine the business records and accounting methods, and to determine whether the correct amount of VAT has been paid and whether returns are completed on time.

Usually there will be a set date agreed with the officer for the visit but on occasions an officer may arrive unannounced in order to see the day-to-day operations of the business.

If the officer believes that VAT has been underpaid, HMRC will raise an assessment requesting payment of the VAT due. If the trader disagrees with the assessment, an appeals procedure is in place to deal with the dispute.

CONTACTING HMRC AND CLIENTS

For assessment criteria 2.2 and 2.3 (Preparing and completing VAT returns), candidates are required to communicate effectively with clients (or colleagues within a business) or HMRC. Whenever contact is made with HMRC officers this must always be done in a polite and professional manner. Similarly, a professional approach should also be adopted with clients and other colleagues.

Much of the information covered in this chapter is available to view throughout the live assessment within the reference material. You should familiarise yourself with this document (included at the back of this Text) and practise using it when attempting any Tasks.

CHAPTER OVERVIEW

- Changes in VAT legislation can have significant impact on accounting systems

- Staff and customers need to be informed of a change to the VAT rate

- The main contact for advice and help for any VAT-registered business is the VAT Helpline

Keyword

VAT Helpline – a helpline available to deal with general enquiries and to give advice

TEST YOUR LEARNING

Test 1

You are a trainee accounting technician working for a sole trader, Mr Smith. Mr Smith has just received a letter from a client, Michael James, who is a trader making only standard-rated supplies to non-registered clients, asking about the impact of the recent change in the standard rate of VAT on his clients. The rate changed from 17.5% to 20%. He is undecided about whether to change his prices.

You are required to draft a letter to Michael James discussing the options open to him.

ANSWERS TO CHAPTER TASKS

CHAPTER 1   The VAT system

Task 1

	Input tax ✓	Output tax ✓
Business A		✓
Business B	✓	

Task 2

	✓
Input tax will increase	
Input tax will decrease	
Output tax will increase	
Output tax will decrease	✓

CHAPTER 2 Accounting for VAT

Task 1

The correct three items that must be included on a valid VAT invoice are:

- Supplier VAT registration number
- Total VAT-exclusive amount
- Total VAT amount

Task 2

	✓
Input tax will increase	✓
Input tax will decrease	
Output tax will increase	
Output tax will decrease	

Task 3

	True ✓	False ✓
A 'less detailed' invoice can be used to reclaim input VAT	✓	
A 'pro forma' invoice can be used to reclaim input VAT		✓

Task 4

	✓
15 May 20X0	
20 May 20X0	✓
20 June 20X0	

Basic tax point	15 May 20X0
Invoice date	20 May 20X0
Payment date	20 June 20X0
Is payment or invoice earlier than basic tax point?	No – so this does not create an actual tax point
Is invoice within 14 days of basic tax point?	Yes – so invoice date overrides basic tax point
TAX POINT	**20 May – actual**

Task 5

	✓
2 June 20X0	✓
11 June 20X0	✓
29 June 20X0	
31 July 20X0	

Tax point

	10% deposit	*Balancing payment*
Basic tax point	11 June 20X0	11 June 20X0
Invoice date	29 June 20X0	29 June 20X0
Payment date	2 June 20X0	31 July 20X0
Is payment or invoice earlier than basic tax point?	Yes – payment 2 June 20X0	No – both later
Is invoice within 14 days of basic tax point?	No	No
TAX POINT	**2 June – actual**	**11 June – basic**

CHAPTER 3   Types of supply

Task 1

The correct answers are:

Business type	Type of supply made	Net cost £
Insurance company	Only exempt supplies	1,200
Accountancy firm	Only standard rated supplies	1,000
Bus company	Only zero rated supplies	1,000

Although the accountancy firm and bus company pay £1,200 for their telephone bills, they are able to reclaim the input VAT of £200, so the net cost is £1,000. The insurance company making exempt supplies is not able to reclaim input tax and so the net cost is £1,200.

Task 2

To registered traders	To non-registered traders	✓
Zero-rated	Zero-rated	
Standard-rated	Zero-rated	
Zero-rated	Standard-rated	✓
Standard-rated	Standard-rated	

Task 3

	✓
No VAT is charged by the EU supplier therefore can be ignored by Joe on his VAT return	
Joe must pay output VAT to HMRC at the port/airport and can reclaim input VAT on the next return	
Joe must charge himself 'output VAT' and 'reclaim input' VAT on the same return	✓

CHAPTER 4   VAT registration and deregistration

Task 1

The correct answer is 30 April 2011.

VAT registration is required when TAXABLE supplies (standard plus zero-rated supplies) exceed £73,000. Taxable supplies are £8,920 (£7,850 + £1,070) per month.

Amy exceeds this threshold after 9 months, ie by 30 April 2011 as taxable supplies are then £80,280 (9 × £8,920).

Task 2

	✓
Preparation of VAT returns would be optional	
Customers would benefit by being able to claim back input VAT	
Business would benefit by being able to claim back input VAT	✓

Once registered, even voluntarily, VAT returns will have to be completed.

VAT-registered customers would neither gain nor lose because they could reclaim VAT charged to them, and non-registered customers would be disadvantaged because they would be charged VAT they could not reclaim.

CHAPTER 5   Output tax and input tax

Task 1

Net £	VAT rate %	VAT £	Gross £
43.50	20	8.70	52.20
18.00	5	0.90	18.90

VAT =   £52.20 × 1/6   VAT =   £18.90 × 1/21

       =   £8.70   =   £0.90

Task 2

	✓
£200.00	
£196.00	
£160.00	
£156.80	✓

	£
Goods total	1,000
Less: trade discount	200
	800
Less: settlement discount	16
	784

VAT £784.00 × 20% = £156.80

Task 3

	✓
The amount payable will increase	
The amount payable will decrease	✓

Task 4

	True ✓	False ✓
A registered business can reclaim all the input VAT attributed to zero-rated supplies.	✓	
A registered business can reclaim all the input VAT attributed to standard-rated supplies	✓	
A registered business can reclaim all the input VAT attributed to exempt supplies		✓
A registered business can reclaim all the input VAT attributed to both taxable and exempt supplies providing certain de minimis tests are satisfied	✓	

CHAPTER 6   VAT return

Task 1

	✓
Input tax paid at the ports is reclaimed as input tax on the VAT return	
They are shown as both input tax and output tax on the VAT return	✓
They are zero-rated and so do not feature on the VAT return	
They are exempt and so do not feature on the VAT return	

Task 2

	✓
VAT charged at the fuel scale rate increases output VAT and is shown in Box 1	✓
VAT on EU acquisitions increases both input VAT and output VAT and is shown in boxes 1 & 4	
Credit notes received from suppliers reduce input VAT and are shown in box 4	✓
Credit notes issued to customers reduce output VAT and are shown in box 1	✓

VAT on EU acquisitions increases both input VAT and output VAT but is shown in boxes 2 & 4

Task 3

To: Finance Director
From: Accounting Technician
Date: 25 April 20XX
Subject: VAT return to 31 March 20XX

Please be advised that I have now completed the VAT return for the quarter to 31 March 20XX. If you are in agreement with the figures shown in the return please could you arrange an electronic payment of **£2,353.30** to be made by **7 May 20XX**.

If you wish to discuss this further please feel free to call me.

Kind regards

CHAPTER 7 Schemes for small businesses

Task 1

	True	False
The first payment due to HMRC is by 1 April 2012.		✓

The first payment due to HMRC is by 30 April 2012 (ie the END of month 4).

Task 2

	✓
Yes, because they would be able to reclaim input VAT earlier	
Yes, because they would pay output VAT later	
No, because they would reclaim input VAT later	✓
No, because they would pay output VAT earlier	

Task 3

	✓
£2,550	
£3,060	✓

The VAT due to HMRC is 8.5% of the VAT inclusive figure.

(£30,000 × 120%) × 8.5% = £3,060

CHAPTER 8   Errors and penalties

Task 1

	✓
A correction can be made on the next VAT return as the error is less than 1% of turnover	
A correction cannot be made on the next return as the error exceeds £10,000	
A correction cannot be made on the next return as the error exceeds £50,000	✓

The error is less than 1% of turnover, but that is subject to an overall limit of £50,000.

Task 2

	✓
An increase in the VAT payable via the current return	✓
A decrease in the VAT payable via the current return	
No impact on the current return. It must just be separately declared	

Task 3

	✓
No – not shown on the return	
Yes – shown in box 1	✓
Yes – shown in box 4	

It is shown as an increase in the output tax at box 1 on the VAT return.

CHAPTER 9 Contact with clients and HMRC

Task 1

VAT inclusive £	VAT rate	VAT exclusive £
235.00	17.5%	200.00
235.00	20 %	195.83

- VAT rate of 17.5% (VAT fraction 7/47 or 17.5/117.5)

  VAT exclusive value £200 (7/47 × £235)

- VAT rate of 20% (VAT fraction 1/6 or 20/120)

  VAT exclusive value £195.83 (1/6 × £235)

TEST YOUR LEARNING – ANSWERS

CHAPTER 1   The VAT system

Test 1

	✓
HM Customs and Excise	
Inland Revenue	
HM Revenue and Customs	✓
HM Treasury	

Test 2

	✓
Output VAT is the VAT charged by a supplier on the sales that are made by his business. Output VAT is collected by the supplier and paid over to HMRC.	✓
Output VAT is the VAT suffered by the purchaser of the goods which will be reclaimed from HMRC if the purchaser is VAT registered and a valid VAT invoice is held.	

The other statement describes input VAT.

Test 3

VAT is collected by HMRC throughout the manufacturing chain for goods. Each business that buys, processes and then sells the goods pays the difference between the VAT on their sale and the VAT on their purchase over to HMRC.

Test 4

	✓
1 year	
2 years	
6 years	✓
20 years	

CHAPTER 2 Accounting for VAT

Test 1

	✓
A pro forma invoice is always sent out when goods are sent to customers, before issuing the proper invoice	
A pro forma invoice always includes the words 'This is not a VAT invoice'	✓
A customer can reclaim VAT stated on a pro forma invoice	
A pro forma invoice is sent out to offer a customer the chance to purchase the goods detailed	✓

Test 2

	Date	Basic/ Actual
An invoice is sent out to a customer for goods on 22 June 20X0 and the goods are dispatched on 29 June 20X0	22 June	A
Goods are sent out to a customer on 18 June 20X0 and this is followed by an invoice on 23 June 20X0	23 June	A
A customer pays in full for goods on 27 June 20X0 and they are then delivered to the customer on 2 July 20X0.	27 June	A

Test 3

VAT CONTROL ACCOUNT

VAT deductible	£	VAT payable	£
Purchases day book	6,344.03	Sales day book	9,147.96
Cash payments book	936.58	Cash receipts book	1,662.78
	7,280.61		10,810.74
Purchases returns day book	(663.57)	Sales returns day book	(994.67)
Total VAT deductible	6,617.04	Total VAT payable	9,816.07
		Less: VAT deductible	(6,617.04)
		Due to HMRC	3,199.03

Test 4

	True ✓	False ✓
If input VAT is greater than output VAT on the return VAT is payable to HMRC		✓
If output VAT is greater than input VAT on the return, VAT is repayable from HMRC		✓

If input VAT is greater than output VAT on the return then VAT is repayable, and if output VAT is greater than input VAT on the return, then VAT is payable to HMRC

CHAPTER 3   Types of supply

Test 1

- ■   Outside the scope of VAT
- ■   Exempt supplies
- ■   Taxable supplies

Test 2

20	%
5	%
0	%

Test 3

	True ✓	False ✓
If a business supplies zero-rated services then the business is not able to reclaim the VAT on its purchases and expenses from HMRC.		✓
A business makes zero-rated supplies. The cost to the business of its purchases and expenses is the VAT exclusive amount.	✓	

Test 4

	✓
The goods will be treated as standard-rated in the UK if the American business is VAT-registered	
The goods will be treated as standard-rated in the UK provided documentary evidence of the export is obtained within three months	
The goods will be treated as zero-rated in the UK if the American business is VAT-registered	
The goods will be treated as zero-rated in the UK provided documentary evidence of the export is obtained within three months	✓

CHAPTER 4   VAT registration and deregistration

Test 1

		Register now	Monitor and register later
A	An existing business with total turnover for the previous 11 months of £70,000. Sales for the next month are unknown at present.		✓
B	A new business with an expected turnover for the next 12 months of £6,250 per month.		✓
C	An existing business with total turnover for the previous 12 months of £6,300 per month.	✓	

Test 2

AN Accountant
Number Street
London
SW11 8AB

Mrs Quirke
Alphabet Street
London
W12 6WM

Dear Mrs Quirke
VAT REGISTRATION

Further to our recent telephone conversation, set out below are the circumstances when you must register your business for VAT.

If the taxable turnover of your business at the end of a month, looking back no more than **twelve** months, has exceeded the registration limit of **£73,000**, then the business must apply to register for VAT.

Alternatively, if at any time, the taxable turnover (before any VAT is added) is expected to exceed the registration limit within the next **30 days** alone, then the business must apply to be registered for VAT. This would be the situation if, for example, you obtained a large one-off contract for, say, £75,000.

If you wish to discuss this in any more detail please do not hesitate to contact me.

Yours sincerely

AN Accountant

CHAPTER 5   Output tax and input tax

Test 1

(a)

The VAT is £	76.80

VAT   =   £384.00 × 20%

           =   £76.80

(b) Which business will treat it as output tax and which will treat it as input tax?

	Output tax ✓	Input tax ✓
Business C	✓	
Business D		✓

Test 2

	✓
Staff party	
Car for sales manager	✓
Photocopier	
Entertaining UK clients	✓

Test 3

	£
A VAT-exclusive list price of £356.75 will have VAT of	71.35
A VAT-exclusive list price of £269.00 where a trade discount of 15 % is given will have VAT of	45.73
A VAT-exclusive list price of £250.00 where a 2.5% settlement discount is offered will have VAT of	48.75
A VAT-exclusive list price of £300.00 where a trade discount of 10% is given and a 3% settlement discount is offered, but not taken up will have VAT of	52.38

(i)   £356.75 × 20%   =   £71.35

(ii)   (£269.00 – £40.35) × 20%   =   £45.73

(iii)   (£250.00 – £6.25) × 20%   =   £48.75

(iv)   (£300.00 – £30.00 – £8.10) × 20%   =   £52.38

Test 4

VAT inclusive	VAT at 20 %
£	£
42.88	7.14
96.57	16.09
28.20	4.70
81.07	13.51

(i)	£42.88 × 1/6	=	£7.14
(ii)	£96.57 × 1/6	=	£16.09
(iii)	£28.20 × 1/6	=	£4.70
(iv)	£81.07 × 1/6	=	£13.51

Test 5

The VAT on a bad debt can be reclaimed from HMRC when the following three conditions are met:

- The debt is more than six months overdue
- The original VAT on the invoice has been paid to HMRC
- The debt is written-off in the accounts of the business

CHAPTER 6   VAT return

Test 1

WORKINGS   £

Box 1

VAT on sales from the sales day book	9,053.48
VAT on sales from the cash receipts book	1,010.92
Less: VAT on credit notes issued	(154.71)
	9,909.69

Box 2

VAT on EU acquisitions	451.21

Box 4

VAT on purchases from purchases day book	6,125.51
VAT on purchases from cash payments book	670.55
VAT on EU acquisitions	451.21
Less: VAT on credit notes received	(142.84)
	7,104.43

Box 6

Zero-rated credit sales	13,447.67
Standard-rated credit sales	45,267.40
Cash sales	5,054.60
Less: zero-rated credit notes	(225.83)
standard-rated credit notes	(773.56)
	62,770

Box 7   £

Zero-rated credit purchases	7,447.30
Standard-rated credit purchases	30,627.55
Cash purchases	3,352.75
EU acquisitions	2,256.07
Less: zero rated credit notes	(215.61)
standard-rated credit notes	(714.20)
	42,753

Box 8   '0'

Box 9

Purchases from EU countries	2,256

VAT due in this period on **sales** and other outputs (Box 1)

9,909.69

VAT due in this period on **acquisitions** from other **EC Member States** (Box 2)

451.21

Total VAT due **(the sum of boxes 1 and 2)** (Box 3)

10,360.90

VAT reclaimed in the period on **purchases** and other inputs, including acquisitions from the EC (Box 4)

7,104.43

Net VAT to be paid to HM Revenue & Customs or reclaimed by you **(Difference between boxes 3 and 4)** (Box 5)

3,256.47

Total value of **sales** and all other outputs excluding any VAT. **Include your box 8 figure** (Box 6)

62,770

Whole pounds only

Total value of purchases and all other inputs excluding any VAT. **Include your box 9 figure** (Box 7)

42,753

Whole pounds only

Total value of all **supplies** of goods and related costs, excluding any VAT, to other **EC Member States** (Box 8)

0

Whole pounds only

Total value of all **acquisitions** of goods and related costs, excluding any VAT, from other **EC Member States** (Box 9)

2,256

Whole pounds only

Test 2

Return	Date	Payment	Date
Paper return	30 June 20X0	Cheque	30 June 20X0
Online return	7 July 20X0	BACs	7 July 20X0
Online return	7 July 20X0	Direct debit	10 July 20X0

CHAPTER 7   Schemes for small businesses

Test 1

> AN accountant
> Number Street
> London
> SW11 8AB

Mr Lymstock
Alphabet Street
London
W12 6WM

Dear Mr Lymstock
ANNUAL ACCOUNTING SCHEME

I have recently been reviewing your files. I would like to make you aware of a scheme that you could use for VAT.

As the annual value of your taxable supplies, **excluding** VAT and supplies of capital items, in the following 12 months is expected to be **below £1,350,000** you can join the annual accounting scheme.

Under this scheme you make **9** monthly direct debit payments based upon an estimate of the amount of VAT due. The first of these payments is due at the end of the **fourth** month of the accounting period. You must then prepare a VAT return for the year and submit it in with the balancing payment, by **two months** after the year end.

Use of this annual accounting scheme is a great help as it means that you only have to prepare **one** VAT return(s) each year.

If you wish to discuss this with me in more detail please do not hesitate to contact me.

Your sincerely

AN Accountant

Test 2

If the annual value of taxable supplies, **excluding** VAT, is **less** than £1,350,000 and provided that a trader has a clean record with HMRC, he may be able to apply to use the cash accounting scheme.

The scheme allows the accounting for VAT to be based upon the date of **receipt and payment of money**. This is particularly useful for a business which gives its customers a **long** period of credit whilst paying its suppliers promptly.

The scheme also gives automatic relief from **bad debts** so if the customer does not pay the amount due, then the VAT need not be accounted for to HMRC.

Test 3

	✓
£897.00	
£1,092.50	
£1,311.00	✓

£9,500 × 120 % × 11.5% = £1,311.00

	✓
More VAT is payable not using the flat rate scheme	
More VAT is payable using the flat rate scheme	✓

If not using the flat rate scheme the VAT payable would be:

		£
Output tax	£9,500 × 20%	1,900.00
Input tax	£3,000 × 20%	(600.00)
		1,300.00

CHAPTER 8   Errors and penalties

Test 1

The correct statement is:

	✓
If a net error of more than the lower of £10,000 and 1% of turnover (subject to an overall £5,000 limit) is discovered it must be disclosed on Form VAT 652	
If a net error of more than the greater of £10,000 and 1% of turnover (subject to an overall £5,000 limit) is discovered it must be disclosed on Form VAT 652.	
If a net error of more than the lower of £10,000 and 1% of turnover (subject to an overall £50,000 limit) is discovered it must be disclosed on Form VAT 652.	
If a net error of more than the greater of £10,000 and 1% of turnover (subject to an overall £50,000 limit) is discovered it must be disclosed on Form VAT 652.	✓

Test 2

True ✓	False ✓
	✓

Tax **evasion** is illegal and could lead to fines and/or imprisonment, as opposed to tax **avoidance**.

Test 3

VAT ACCOUNT

VAT deductible	£	VAT payable	£
Purchases day book	1,825.67	Sales day book	3,572.15
Cash payments book	514.37	Cash receipts book	994.67
EU acquisitions	236.57	EU acquisitions	236.57
Bad debt relief	105.37	Undercharge of output VAT	44.79
Underclaim of input VAT	25.47		
Total VAT deductible	2,707.45	Total VAT payable	4,848.18
		Less: VAT deductible	–2,707.45
		Due to HMRC	2,140.73

CHAPTER 9   Contact with clients and HMRC

Test 1

Mr Smith
Number Street
London
SW11 8AB

Mr James
Alphabet Street
London
W12 6WM

Dear Mr James
CHANGE IN THE STANDARD RATE OF VAT

Further to your recent letter, I have set out below the options open to you in relation to the recent change in the standard rate of VAT.

Until recently you have been charging VAT at a rate of 17.5%. Therefore a VAT-exclusive sale with a value of £1,000 has cost your non-registered clients £1,175 (£1,000 plus VAT of £175).

The two options open to you are as follows:

- Keep the same VAT-exclusive value of £1,000

    The benefit of this option is that you have the same amount of VA-exclusive sales value per item sold. However, this will now make the VA-inclusive cost to your customers higher at £1,200 (£1,000 plus VAT at 20%). This may makes your prices less competitive (if your competitors do not do the same) and may result in a loss of some customers.

- Keep the same VAT-inclusive value of £1,175

    Under this alternative option you will remain competitive to your customers. However, your VAT-exclusive sales value per item sold will be reduced to £979.16 (£1,175 × 100/120).

There is no obvious correct option to choose, it will depend primarily on the strength of your competitors.

If you wish to discuss this with me in more detail please do not hesitate to contact me.

Your sincerely

Mr Smith

Question bank

Indirect Tax Question Bank

Chapter 1

Task 1.1

On 1 June, Black Ltd receives goods from a supplier, and also receives an invoice that includes VAT.

In preparing Black Ltd's VAT return is this amount of VAT to be treated as output VAT or input VAT (insert a tick)?

Output tax

Input tax

Task 1.2

Complete the sentence below by writing in the appropriate word.

A trader must retain a valid VAT		in order to reclaim input tax.

Task 1.3

It is important for a VAT-registered trader to complete VAT returns regularly.

Complete the sentence below by writing in the appropriate number.

Most VAT-registered traders must complete a VAT return every		months.

Task 1.4

Mr Green is a VAT-registered trader making standard-rated, zero-rated and exempt supplies.

Is he required to retain records of the amounts of different categories of supplies for VAT purposes (insert ticks)?

	Yes	No
Standard-rated supplies		
Zero-rated supplies		
Exempt supplies		

Task 1.5

A VAT-registered trader is required to keep adequate records to calculate the VAT due or reclaimable.

Complete the sentence below by writing in the appropriate number.

VAT records should usually be retained for		years.

Task 1.6

Mrs Violet is VAT-registered and runs a business making both cash and credit sales and purchases.

In order to calculate the correct amount of output tax for Mrs Violet's business, which of the following accounting records will be needed (insert ticks)?

	Yes	No
Sales day book		
Purchases day book		
Cash receipts book		
Cash payments book		

Task 1.7

Mrs Orange is VAT-registered and runs a business making both cash and credit sales and purchases.

In order to calculate the correct amount of input tax for Mrs Orange's business, which of the following accounting records will be needed (insert ticks)?

	Yes	No
Sales day book		
Purchases day book		
Cash receipts book		
Cash payments book		
Sales returns day book		
Purchases returns day book		

Chapter 2

Task 2.1

Identify which of the following details would not need to appear on a less detailed VAT invoice for a retail sale of less than £250.00.

A   The supplier's name and address
B   The date of supply
C   Description of the goods/ services
D   The total excluding VAT

Task 2.2

Clipper Ltd holds the following invoices from suppliers.

(a)

VAT reg no 446 9989 57			Jupiter plc
Date: 4 January 20X0			1 London Road
Tax point: 4 January 20X0			Reading
Invoice no.			RL3 7CM
Clippers Ltd			
13 Gale Road			
Chester-le-Street			
NE1 1LB			
Sales of goods			
Type	*Quantity*	*VAT rate*	*Net*
		%	£
Earrings @ £0.5 per unit	2,700	20	1,350.00
Earring studs @ £0.5 per unit	2,800	20	1,400.00
			2,750.00
VAT at 20%			522.50
Payable within 60 days			3,272.50
Less 5% discount if paid within 14 days			137.50
			3,135.00

(b)

HILLSIDE LTD

'The Glasgow Based Supplier of Quality Jewellery Items'

VAT reg no 337 4849 26

Clipper Ltd

13 Gale Road

Chester-le-Street

NE1 1LB

Invoice no. 0010

Date: 10 August 20X0

Tax point: 10 August 20X0

	£
Sale of 4,000 Jewellery boxes @ £2 per unit	8,000
VAT at 20%	1,600
Total	9,600

Terms: strictly net 30 days

(c)

GENEROUS PLC

11 Low Fell

Leeds

LS1 XY2

Clipper Ltd

13 Gale Road

Chester-le-Street

NE1 1LB

Invoice no: 2221

Date: 12 December 20X0

Tax point: 12 December 20X0

	Net	VAT	Total
	£	£	£
4,000 Earrings @ £0.5 per unit	2,000.00	400.00	2,400.00
8,000 Brooches @ £0.3125 per unit	2,500.00	500.00	3,000.00
2,500 'How to make Jewellery' books @ £2 per book	5,000.00	0.00	5,000.00
	9,500.00	900.00	10,400.00

(d)

JEWELS & CO

101 High Street, Gateshead NE2 22P

VAT reg no 499 3493 27

Date: 2 February 20X0

30 necklaces sold for £4 each totalling £120.00 including VAT at 20%.

For each of the above invoices, state whether it is a valid VAT invoice. If it is not valid identify the missing item(s).

Choose from the following:

[Supplier's address, Invoice number, Supplier's VAT registration number, Applicable rates of VAT (0% & 20%)]

Invoice	Valid	Not valid	Missing item (s)
(a)			
(b)			
(c)			
(d)			

Task 2.3

Identify which one of the following statements would need to appear on a pro forma invoice.

A   THIS IS A PRO FORMA INVOICE
B   THIS IS NOT A VAT INVOICE
C   THIS INVOICE DOES NOT ALLOW INPUT VAT RECOVERY
D   THESE GOODS HAVE NOT YET BEEN DELIVERED

Task 2.4

Mr Glass has sent a credit note to a customer.

As a result of issuing this credit note, will Mr Glass have to pay more or less VAT to HMRC (insert a tick)?

More VAT payable	
Less VAT payable	

Task 2.5

Miss Spoon has received a credit note from a supplier.

Which ONE of the following is the effect on VAT?

A   Output tax will increase
B   Output tax will decrease
C   Input tax will increase
D   Input tax will decrease

Task 2.6

An invoice is dispatched to a customer on 13 August and the goods are delivered the following day.

What is the tax point in this situation and is it a basic tax point or an actual tax point?

A   13 August and actual tax point
B   13 August and basic tax point
C   14 August and actual tax point
D   14 August and basic tax point

Task 2.7

A customer orders goods on 13 August. The goods are delivered on 15 August and the invoice is sent to the customer on 31 August. Payment for the goods is made on 15 September.

What is the tax point of this transaction?

A   13 August
B   15 August
C   31 August
D   15 September

Task 2.8

If the column for input tax is greater than the column for output tax in the VAT account, this will result in:

TICK ONE BOX

	✓
a VAT payment due to HMRC	
a VAT repayment from HMRC	

Task 2.9

Given below is information about the VAT of a business that has been taken from the books of prime entry:

VAT figures

	£
From the sales day book	3,474.89
From the sales returns day book	441.46
From the purchases day book	2,485.61
From the purchases returns day book	210.68
From the cash receipts book	993.57
From the cash payments book	624.78

Write up the VAT account

VAT account

Details	Amount £	Details	Amount £

Narratives

Sales day book
Sales returns day book
Purchases day book
Purchases returns day book
Cash receipts book
Cash payments book
Total VAT payable
Total VAT deductible
Less: VAT deductible
Due to HMRC
Less: VAT payable
Reclaimed from HMRC

Chapter 3

Task 3.1

Identify which of the following types of supply are deemed to be taxable supplies for VAT purposes.

A   Standard-rated supplies only
B   Standard and zero-rated supplies
C   Zero-rated and exempt supplies
D   All three types of supply

Task 3.2

Several businesses each purchased goods during a month for £13,500 plus VAT.

Identify whether each of these businesses can reclaim the input tax on the goods purchased (insert ticks).

	Reclaim	No reclaim
Bread Ltd – making only standard-rated supplies		
Soup Ltd – making only exempt supplies		
Marmalade Ltd – making only zero-rated supplies		

Task 3.3

Jam Ltd is a bus company making only zero-rated supplies.

Which one of the following statements is correct in relation to Jam Ltd (insert a tick)?

	Correct
Jam Ltd cannot register for VAT	
If Jam Ltd is VAT-registered it will make payments to HMRC	
If Jam Ltd is VAT-registered it will have repayments from HMRC	

Task 3.4

Mohammed has purchased goods from a supplier in another EU country.

This purchase is known as which ONE of the following?

A   Import
B   Export
C   Acquisition
D   Despatch

Task 3.5

James is selling goods to a VAT-registered trader in another EU country.

In order for this to be treated as zero-rated, what information about the customer should be included on the sales invoice?

A   No information required
B   Name and VAT registration number only
C   Name and address only
D   Name, address and VAT registration number

Task 3.6

Lucinda is exporting goods to a customer in India, which is outside the EU.

Complete the sentence below by writing in the appropriate word(s).

Goods exported to customers outside the EU must be treated as	

Picklist:

Outside the scope of VAT
Standard-rated
Zero-rated
Exempt

Task 3.7

Jones Ltd, a VAT-registered business, which makes standard-rated supplies, imports goods from outside the EU. The goods would be standard-rated with VAT of £3,100 if supplied in the UK.

Which one of the following is the net VAT position for Jones Ltd (insert a tick)?

	Correct
VAT payable to HMRC of £3,100	
VAT reclaimed from HMRC of £3,100	
Nil net VAT effect	

Task 3.8

A UK registered business acquires goods from another EU country.

Which ONE of the following statements is correct?

TICK ONE BOX

	✓
As long as the UK business supplies its VAT number to the EU supplier the goods will be zero rated and VAT doesn't need to be accounted for	
The UK business will charge itself output tax for the goods on the VAT return and reclaim input tax on the same return	
The UK business will pay output tax to HMRC at the point of entry into the UK and reclaim input tax on the next return	
The EU supplier will charge VAT on the goods and the UK business will be able to reclaim the VAT on its next return	

Chapter 4

Task 4.1

Bradley's business makes taxable supplies of approximately £30,000 each year. He is considering voluntarily registering for VAT.

Identify whether the following statements are true or false in relation to voluntary registration (insert a tick).

	True	False
If Bradley's business makes zero-rated supplies, it will be in a VAT repayment position		
If Bradley makes standard-rated supplies, it will be disadvantageous for non VAT-registered customers		

Task 4.2

Identify whether the following businesses need to register for VAT immediately, or monitor turnover and register later. (Insert a tick on each line)

	Register now	Monitor and register later
An existing business with a total turnover of £6,000 per month for the last 12 months.		
An new business with an expected turnover of £25,000 per month for the next 12 months		
An existing business with a total turnover of £5,000 per month for the last 12 months. A one off contract will bring in additional sales of £71,000, in 10 days time.		

Task 4.3

Identify whether each of these businesses can VAT register (insert ticks).

	Can register	Cannot register
Blackberry Ltd – making only zero-rated supplies		
Raspberry Ltd – making standard-rated and zero-rated supplies		
Loganberry Ltd – making only exempt supplies		
Gooseberry Ltd – making standard-rated and exempt supplies		

Task 4.4

A VAT-registered trader's sales are looking like they will fall below the deregistration limit.

The trader may deregister if: (fill in the appropriate word)

Taxable turnover in the next		months is expected to fall below the deregistration limit

Task 4.5

The deregistration limit is always less than the registration limit by:

A   £1,000
B   £2,000
C   £5,000
D   £10,000

Chapter 5

Task 5.1

Below are details of two VAT invoices to be issued by a trader who makes only standard-rated supplies.

Insert the figures in the relevant columns, as appropriate.

Invoice number	Net £	VAT £	Gross £
1000325			390.60
1000326	452.92		

Task 5.2

Below are details of the VAT exclusive (net) amounts on two VAT invoices to be issued by a trader who makes only standard-rated supplies (at 20 %).

Invoice 25 – Goods sold for £220.00 less a trade discount of 10%

Invoice 26 – Goods sold for £200.00 with a settlement discount of 3% offered

Insert the figures in the relevant columns, as appropriate.

	Shown on invoice as	
Invoice number	VAT exclusive £	VAT £
25		
26		

Task 5.3

Knife Ltd has not been paid by a customer for an invoice issued some time ago. The company now wishes to claim a refund of the VAT on that invoice from HMRC. It can do so provided certain conditions are fulfilled.

Which one of the following is NOT a relevant condition?

A   Six months must have elapsed since payment was due

B   Output tax has been accounted for and paid

C   Notice must have been received from the customer's liquidators to state that it is insolvent

D   The debt must have been written-off in the accounts of Knife Ltd

Task 5.4

Dish Ltd purchases all of the fuel for cars of the salesmen. The company reclaims the VAT on the fuel purchased. The salesmen also use their cars for private motoring.

Complete the sentence below by writing in the appropriate word.

On the VAT return Dish Ltd must include an amount of		tax to take
account of the private fuel used by salesmen		

Picklist:

output
input

Task 5.5

A VAT-registered business has made the following purchases:

- A car for use by the sales manager for £14,200 plus VAT
- A van for use by the stores man for £10,500 plus VAT

How much VAT can be reclaimed by the business?

A   Nil
B   £2,840.00
C   £2,100.00
D   £4,940.00

Task 5.6

Where a registered business makes a mixture of standard-rated, zero-rated and exempt supplies, which of the following statements is correct?

TICK ONE BOX

	✓
All input tax can be reclaimed	
Only input tax relating to standard-rated supplies can be reclaimed	
All input tax can be reclaimed provided certain de minimis tests are met	
Only input tax relating to standard and zero-rated supplies can be reclaimed	
No input tax can be reclaimed	

Chapter 6

Task 6.1

Given below is information about the VAT of a business taken from the books of prime entry:

	£
From the sales day book	6,275.78
From the sales returns day book	726.58
From the purchases day book	4,668.14
From the purchases returns day book	510.36
From the cash receipts book	1,447.30
From the cash payments book	936.47
EU acquisitions	772.46
Bad debt relief	284.67

You are to write up the VAT account.

VAT account

Details	Amount £	Details	Amount £

Picklist:

Sales day book
Sales returns day book
Purchases day book
Purchases returns day book
Cash receipts book
Cash payments book
EU acquisitions
Bad debt relief
Total VAT payable
Total VAT deductible
EU acquisitions
Less: VAT deductible
Due to HMRC

Less VAT payable
Recoverable from HMRC

Task 6.2

Given below are extracts from the books of prime entry for a business Waltzer Enterprises, Adam Industrial Park, Yarden, LR3 9GS. The business's VAT registration number is 234 4576 12 and the tax period is April 20X0 to June 20X0.

Sales day book summary

	Zero-rated sales	Standard-rated sales	VAT	Total
	£	£	£	£
Total	3,628.47	57,615.80	11,523.16	72,767.43

Purchases day book summary

	Zero-rated purchases	Standard-rated purchases	VAT	Total
	£	£	£	£
EU acquisitions		1,572.45	314.49	1,886.94
UK purchases	2,636.47	33,672.57	6,734.51	43,043.55

Sales returns day book summary

	Zero-rated sales	Standard-rated sales	VAT	Total
	£	£	£	£
Total	236.34	4,782.57	956.51	5,975.42

Purchases returns day book summary

	Zero-rated purchases	Standard-rated purchases	VAT	Total
	£	£	£	£
Total	125.34	3,184.57	636.91	3,946.82

Cash receipts book summary

	Net	VAT	Total
	£	£	£
Cash sales	5,325.65	1,065.13	6,390.78

Cash payments book summary

	Net	VAT	Total
	£	£	£
Cash purchases	3,157.46	631.49	3,788.95

You are required to complete boxes 1 to 9 of the VAT return given.

VAT due in this period on **sales** and other outputs (Box 1)

VAT due in this period on **acquisitions** from other **EC Member States** (Box 2)

Total VAT due (**the sum of boxes 1 and 2**) (Box 3)

VAT reclaimed in the period on **purchases** and other inputs, including acquisitions from the EC (Box 4)

Net VAT to be paid to HM Revenue & Customs or reclaimed by you (**Difference between boxes 3 and 4**) (Box 5)

Total value of **sales** and all other outputs excluding any VAT. **Include your box 8 figure** (Box 6)

Whole pounds only

Total value of purchases and all other inputs excluding any VAT. **Include your box 9 figure** (Box 7)

Whole pounds only

Total value of all **supplies** of goods and related costs, excluding any VAT, to other **EC Member States** (Box 8)

Whole pounds only

Total value of all **acquisitions** of goods and related costs, excluding any VAT, from other **EC Member States** (Box 9)

Whole pounds only

Task 6.3

Camilla's business has sales of approximately £70,000. She has always submitted paper VAT returns.

By what date should the VAT return to 31 May 20X0 be submitted (insert a tick)?

30 June 20X0

7 July 20X0

10 July 20X0

By what date should any tax due for the return to 31 May 20X0 be paid (insert a tick)?

30 June 20X0

7 July 20X0

10 July 20X0

Task 6.4

Cordelia's business has sales of approximately £200,000. She submits her VAT returns online and pays by BACS.

By what date should the VAT return to 31 May 20X0 be submitted (insert a tick)?

30 June 20X0

7 July 20X0

10 July 20X0

By what date should any tax due for the return to 31 May 20X0 be paid (insert a tick)?

30 June 20X0

7 July 20X0

10 July 20X0

Task 6.5

Charlotte's business has sales of approximately £200,000. She submits her VAT returns online and pays her VAT by direct debit.

By what date should the VAT return to 31 May 20X0 be submitted (insert a tick)?

30 June 20X0

7 July 20X0

10 July 20X0

By what date should any tax due for the return to 31 May 20X0 be paid (insert a tick)?

30 June 20X0	
7 July 20X0	
10 July 20X0	

Task 6.6

(a) Happy Ltd is able to reclaim bad debt relief on an unpaid invoice.

Which ONE of the following statements is correct?

	✓
Input tax reclaimable will be increased and the bad debt VAT will be included in box 4 on the VAT return	
Output tax payable will be decreased and the bad debt will VAT be included as a deduction in box 1 on the VAT return	

(b) Unhappy Ltd reclaims all the input tax on petrol provided to an employee for both business and private use, and will account for the private element of this by using the fuel scale charge.

Which ONE of the following statements is correct?

	✓
Output tax payable will be increased and the fuel scale charge will be included in box 1 on the VAT return	
Input tax reclaimable will be decreased and the fuel scale charge will be included as a deduction in box 4 on the VAT return	

Chapter 7

Task 7.1

Declan has heard that there is a special scheme available to some businesses that requires only one VAT return to be prepared each year.

Complete the sentences below by writing in the appropriate words/number.

Businesses submit only one return each year if they operate the		scheme

Picklist:

flat rate
annual accounting
cash accounting

Taxable supplies in the next 12 months must be below £	

Task 7.2

Complete the sentence below by writing in the appropriate words.

A business gets automatic bad debt relief if it operates the		scheme

Picklist:

flat rate
annual accounting
cash accounting

Task 7.3

Harry operates the flat rate scheme for his business.

Complete the sentence below by writing in the appropriate word.

Harry's VAT payable is calculated as a percentage of the VAT		turnover

Picklist:

inclusive
exclusive

Task 7.4

Debbie has a business with a year ended 30 April 20X0. Debbie operates the annual accounting scheme. She submits a paper return.

Which one of the following statements is correct?

A   She pays some of her VAT by monthly instalments with the balance due by 31 May 20X0

B   She pays some of her VAT by monthly instalments with the balance due by 30 June 20X0

C   She pays all of her VAT in a single payment by 31 May 20X0

D   She pays all of her VAT in a single payment by 30 June 20X0

Task 7.5

Donald operates the cash accounting scheme.

Identify whether the following statements are true or false in relation to the cash accounting scheme (insert a tick).

	True	False
VAT is accounted for on the basis of cash paid and received rather than on invoices		
The scheme is advantageous for businesses making only zero rated supplies		
Businesses must leave the scheme if taxable supplies in the previous 12 months exceed £1,350,000		

Task 7.6

Jack operates the flat rate scheme.

Identify whether the following statements are true or false in relation to the flat rate scheme (insert a tick).

	True	False
Businesses issue normal VAT invoices to customers		
VAT is paid in instalments		
The flat rate percentage applied depends on the type of business		
Less VAT may be payable by Jack as a result of operating the scheme		

Task 7.7

Would a business that gives its customers long periods of credit, but pays its suppliers promptly benefit from operating under the cash accounting scheme?

	✓
Yes, because output VAT would be paid later and input VAT would be reclaimed at the same time or earlier	
No, because input VAT would be reclaimed later and output VAT would be paid at the same time or earlier	

Chapter 8

Task 8.1

You have discovered an error on the VAT return of a client. You adjust for this error on the next VAT return if it is:

A More than the error correction reporting threshold, but not deliberate
B Less than the error correction reporting threshold and not deliberate
C More than the error correction reporting threshold and was deliberate
D Less than the error correction reporting threshold, but was deliberate

Task 8.2

Amy's business has made a large error that exceeded the error correction reporting threshold, but was not careless or deliberate.

Identify whether the following statements are true or false in relation to this large error (insert a tick).

	True	False
Amy can adjust this on her next return provided she also informs HMRC in writing of the error		
Amy cannot adjust this error on her next return and will be liable for a penalty		

Task 8.3

A business has made a small understatement of input tax in a previous quarter that is below the error correction threshold. Should this adjustment be shown on the latest VAT return, and if so where on the return?

	✓
No – not shown on the return	
Yes – shown in box 1	
Yes – shown in box 4	

Task 8.4

Peter Perfect runs a retail business supplying both trades people and the general public, and is registered for VAT. He does not use the cash accounting scheme or any retail scheme.

Peter had the following transactions in the quarter ended 31 March 20X0.

Date	Type	Net amount	VAT rate
		£	%
2 January	Sale	6,237	20
4 January	Purchase	9,950	20
4 January	Sale	14,850	0
7 January	Purchase	5,792	20
10 January	Sale	19,008	20
21 January	Sale	2,079	0
2 February	Sale	29,700	0
14 February	Purchases returned	743	20
14 February	Sale	3,416	0
16 February	Purchase	8,168	20
27 February	Sales returned	1,188	0
1 March	Sale	1,084	20
13 March	Purchases returned	178	20
17 March	Sale	2,525	0
31 March	Sales returned	505	20

All returns of goods are evidenced by credit notes for both the net price and (where applicable) the VAT. All returns related to current period transactions, except for the return on 14 February.

On the previous period's VAT return, output VAT was overstated by £700 and input VAT was understated by £800. The net error is below the error correction reporting threshold.

Using the information provided above , you are required to prepare Peter's VAT account for the quarter.

VAT account

Details	Amount £	Details	Amount £

Narratives:

Sales
Sales returns
Purchases
Purchases returns
Understated input tax
Overstated output tax
Total VAT payable
Total VAT deductible
Less VAT deductible
Less VAT payable
Due to HMRC
Due from HMRC

Task 8.5

Adbul has just submitted his VAT return late. He has previously sent in all VAT returns on time.

Which one of the following statements is correct?

A   No action will be taken by HMRC
B   HMRC will issue a surcharge liability notice
C   HMRC will issue a surcharge liability notice and charge a penalty
D   HMRC charge a penalty only

Task 8.6

Complete the sentence below by writing in the appropriate number.

A business has a requirement to retain VAT records for [   ] years.

Task 8.7

Tax avoidance is illegal and consists of seeking to pay too little tax by deliberately misleading HMRC. Is this statement true or false?

	✓
TRUE	
FALSE	

Chapter 9

Task 9.1

Your client is Howard, who is currently VAT-registered. Howard's business is affected by a change in the VAT registration limits. Until now your client has had to be VAT-registered. However, the business has slowed down and the VAT registration/deregistration limits have increased. As a result your client could choose to deregister. The majority of the client's customers are members of the general public and not VAT-registered.

Assume today's date is 1 June 20X0.

Draft an e-mail to your client advising him of the options available to him.

To:

From:

Date:

Subject:

Please be advised that the current level of your business turnover is such that you are

able to VAT   register/deregister.   As you will no longer need to charge   input/output

VAT to your customers, there are two options open to you.

1. Your selling prices can decrease to the VAT-exclusive amount

   As a result your profits will   increase/decrease/stay the same.   At the same time your

   customer will have   the same/ a higher/a lower   cost.

2. Your selling prices can stay at the same VAT-inclusive amount

   As a result your profits will   increase/decrease/stay the same   At the same time your

   customer will have   the same/a higher/a lower   cost.

If you wish to discuss this further please feel free to make an appointment.

Kind regards

Task 9.2

It is 1 October 20X0 and you work for a firm of accountants, ABC & Co. Your client Mr Jones is considering joining the annual accounting scheme. Mr Jones' business operates from Unit 1 Alias Industrial Estate, Chelmsford, Essex, CM2 3FG

You have been asked to complete the letter to Mr Jones explaining how the annual accounting scheme operates.

ABC & Co
2 Smith Street
London
W1 2DE

1 October 20X0

Mr Jones
Unit 1 Alias Industrial Estate,
Chelmsford,
Essex,
CM2 3FG

Dear [   ]

[   ] **(subject)**

Further to our telephone conversation of today, I have set out below the details relating to the annual accounting scheme.

Your business can join the annual accounting scheme if the value of its taxable supplies **(including/ excluding)** VAT, in the forthcoming [   ] months does not exceed £ [   ]

Under this scheme the business usually makes [   ] equal monthly instalments. Each of these instalments is [   ] of the estimated VAT liability. The first payment is due at the **(beginning/ end)** of the [   ] month of the accounting period.

The balancing payment and the VAT return will be sent to HMRC within [   ] **(time period)** of the end of the accounting period.

I hope that this has clarified the position. If you wish to discuss this further please do not hesitate to contact me.

Yours sincerely

Answer bank

Answer bank

Indirect Tax Answer Bank

Chapter 1

Task 1.1

Output tax	
Input tax	

Task 1.2

A trader must retain a valid VAT	invoice	in order to reclaim input tax.

Task 1.3

Most VAT-registered traders must complete a VAT return every	3	months.

Task 1.4

	Yes	No
Standard-rated supplies	✓	
Zero rated-supplies	✓	
Exempt supplies	✓	

Task 1.5

VAT records should usually be retained for	6	years.

Task 1.6

	Yes	No
Sales day book	✓	
Purchases day book		✓
Cash receipts book	✓	
Cash payments book		✓

Task 1.7

	Yes	No
Sales day book		✓
Purchases day book	✓	
Cash receipts book		✓
Cash payments book	✓	
Sales returns day book		✓
Purchases returns day book	✓	

Chapter 2

Task 2.1

D   The total excluding VAT

For each applicable VAT rate the total *including VAT* is required together with the rates.

Task 2.2

Invoice	Valid	Not valid	Missing item (s)
(a)		✓	Invoice number
(b)		✓	Supplier's address
(c)		✓	Supplier's VAT registration number/ Applicable rates of VAT(0% & 20%)
(d)	✓		

Note:

The total value of the supply by Jewels & Co, including VAT, does not exceed £250, so a less detailed invoice is permissible.

The invoice is valid, because it includes all the information which must be shown on a less detailed invoice.

Task 2.3

B   THIS IS NOT A VAT INVOICE

Task 2.4

More VAT payable	
Less VAT payable	✓

Task 2.5

D   Input tax will decrease

Task 2.6

A   13 August and actual tax point

Task 2.7

B   15 August

Task 2.8

	✓
a VAT payment due to HMRC	
a VAT repayment from HMRC	✓

Task 2.9

VAT account

Details	Amount £	Details	Amount £
Purchases day book	2,485.61	Sales day book	3,474.89
Cash payments book	624.78	Cash receipts book	993.57
Purchases returns day book	(210.68)	Sales returns day book	(441.46)
Total VAT deductible	2,899.71	Total VAT payable	4,027.00
		Less: VAT deductible	(2,899.71)
		Due to HMRC	1,127.29

Chapter 3

Task 3.1

B   Standard and zero-rated supplies

Task 3.2

	Reclaim	No reclaim
Bread Ltd – making only standard-rated supplies	✓	
Soup Ltd – making only exempt supplies		✓
Marmalade Ltd – making only zero-rated supplies	✓	

Task 3.3

	Correct
Jam Ltd cannot register for VAT	
If Jam Ltd is VAT-registered it will make payments to HMRC	
If Jam Ltd is VAT-registered it will have repayments from HMRC	✓

Task 3.4

C   Acquisition

Task 3.5

D   Name, address and VAT registration number

Task 3.6

Goods exported to customers outside the EU must be treated as	zero-rated

Task 3.7

	Correct
VAT payable to HMRC of £3,100	
VAT reclaimed from HMRC of £3,100	
Nil net VAT effect	✓

Task 3.8

	✓
As long as the UK business supplies its VAT number to the EU supplier the goods will be zero rated and VAT doesn't need to be accounted for	
The UK business will charge itself output tax for the goods on its VAT return and reclaim input tax on the same return	✓
The UK business will pay output tax to HMRC at the point of entry into the UK and reclaim input tax on the next return	
The EU supplier will charge VAT on the goods and the UK business will be able to reclaim the VAT on its next return	

Chapter 4

Task 4.1

	True	False
If Bradley's business makes zero-rated supplies, it will be in a VAT repayment position.	✓	
If Bradley makes standard-rated supplies, it will be disadvantageous for non VAT-registered customers.	✓	

Task 4.2

	Register now	Monitor and register later
An existing business with a total turnover of £6,000 per month for the last 12 months.		✓
An new business with an expected turnover of £25,000 per month for the next 12 months		✓
An existing business with a total turnover of £5,000 per month for the last 12 months and a one off contract that will bring in additional sales of £71,000, in 10 days time.	✓	

Task 4.3

	Can register	Cannot register
Blackberry Ltd – making only zero-rated supplies	✓	
Raspberry Ltd – making standard-rated and zero-rated supplies	✓	
Loganberry Ltd – making only exempt supplies		✓
Gooseberry Ltd – making standard-rated and exempt supplies	✓	

Task 4.4

Taxable turnover in the next	12	months is expected to fall below the deregistration limit

Task 4.5

B   £2,000

Chapter 5

Task 5.1

Invoice number	Net £	VAT £	Gross £
1000325	325.50	65.10	390.60
1000326	452.92	90.58	543.50

Task 5.2

	Shown on invoice as:	
Invoice number	VAT exclusive £	VAT £
25	198.00	39.60
26	200.00	38.80 *

* Full VAT exclusive amount shown on the invoice BUT VAT calculated as if the settlement discount will be taken

£(200.00 × 97%) × 20%

Task 5.3

C   Notice must have been received from the customer's liquidators to state that it is insolvent

Task 5.4

On the VAT return Dish Ltd must include an amount of	output	tax to take
account of the private fuel used by salesmen		

Task 5.5

C   £2,100.00

VAT is irrecoverable on cars purchased with both business and private use.

Task 5.6

	✓
All input tax can be reclaimed	
Only input tax relating to standard rated supplies can be reclaimed	
All input tax can be reclaimed provided certain de minimis tests are met	✓
Only input tax relating to standard and zero rated supplies can be reclaimed	
No input tax can be reclaimed	

Chapter 6

Task 6.1

VAT account

Details	Amount £	Details	Amount £
Purchases day book	4,668.14	Sales day book	6,275.78
Cash payments book	936.47	Cash receipts book	1,447.30
EU acquisitions	772.46	EU acquisitions	772.46
Bad debt relief	284.67		
Purchases returns day book	(510.36)	Sales returns day book	(726.58)
Total VAT deductible	6,151.38	Total VAT payable	7,768.96
		Less: VAT deductible	(6,151.38)
		Due to HMRC	1,617.58

Task 6.2

VAT due in this period on **sales** and other outputs (Box 1)

11,631.78

VAT due in this period on **acquisitions** from other **EC Member States** (Box 2)

314.49

Total VAT due (**the sum of boxes 1 and 2)** (Box 3)

11,946.27

VAT reclaimed in the period on **purchases** and other inputs, including acquisitions from the EC (Box 4)

7,043.58

Net VAT to be paid to HM Revenue & Customs or reclaimed by you (**Difference between boxes 3 and 4)** (Box 5)

4,902.69

Total value of **sales** and all other outputs excluding any VAT. **Include your box 8 figure** (Box 6)

61,551

Whole pounds only

Total value of purchases and all other inputs excluding any VAT. **Include your box 9 figure** (Box 7)

37,728

Whole pounds only

Total value of all **supplies** of goods and related costs, excluding any VAT, to other **EC Member States** (Box 8)

0

Whole pounds only

Total value of all **acquisitions** of goods and related costs, excluding any VAT, from other **EC Member States** (Box 9)

1,572

Whole pounds only

Workings

		£
Box 1	Sales day book	11,523.16
	Cash receipts book	1,065.13
	Sales returns day book	(956.51)
		11,631.78
Box 4	Purchases day book – EU	314.49
	Purchases day book – UK	6,734.51
	Cash payments book	631.49
	Purchases returns day book	(636.91)
		7,043.58
Box 6	Sales day book – zero-rated	3,628.47
	Sales day book – standard-rated	57,615.80
	Cash receipts book	5,325.65
	Sales returns day book – zero-rated	(236.34)
	Sales returns – standard-rated	(4,782.57)
		61,551.01
Box 7	Purchases day book – EU	1,572.45
	Purchases day book – zero-rated	2,636.47
	Purchases day book – standard-rated	33,672.57
	Cash payments book	3,157.46
	Purchases returns – zero-rated	(125.34)
	Purchases returns – standard-rated	(3,184.57)
		37,729.04

Task 6.3

VAT return to 31 May 20X0 submission date

30 June 20X0	✓
7 July 20X0	
10 July 20X0	

VAT due

30 June 20X0	✓
7 July 20X0	
10 July 20X0	

Task 6.4

VAT return to 31 May 20X0 submission date

30 June 20X0	
7 July 20X0	✓
10 July 20X0	

VAT due

30 June 20X0	
7 July 20X0	✓
10 July 20X0	

Task 6.5

VAT return to 31 May 20X0 submission date

30 June 20X0	
7 July 20X0	✓
10 July 20X0	

VAT due

30 June 20X0	
7 July 20X0	
10 July 20X0	✓

Task 6.6

(a)

	✓
Input tax reclaimable will be increased and the bad debt VAT will be included in box 4 on the VAT return	✓
Output tax payable will be decreased and the bad debt VAT will be included as a deduction in box 1 on the VAT return	

(b)

	✓
Output tax payable will be increased and the fuel scale charge will be included in box 1 on the VAT return	✓
Input tax reclaimable will be decreased and the fuel scale charge will be included as a deduction in box 4 on the VAT return	

Chapter 7

Task 7.1

Businesses submit only 1 return each year if they operate the	**annual accounting**	scheme

Taxable supplies in the next 12 months must be below £	**1,350,000**

Task 7.2

A business gets automatic bad debt relief if it operates the	**cash accounting**	scheme

Task 7.3

Harry's VAT payable is calculated as a percentage of the VAT	**inclusive**	turnover

Task 7.4

B   She pays some of her VAT by monthly instalments with the balance due by 30 June 20X0

Task 7.5

	True	False
VAT is accounted for on the basis of cash paid and received rather than on invoices	✓	
The scheme is advantageous for businesses making only zero rated supplies		✓*
Businesses must leave the scheme if taxable supplies in the previous 12 months exceed £1,350,000		✓**

*   Input tax is generally reclaimed later under the cash accounting scheme, so this is not advantageous

**   The limit for leaving is £1,600,000

Task 7.6

	True	False
Businesses issue normal VAT invoices to customers	✓	
VAT is paid in instalments		✓
The flat rate percentage applied depends on the type of business	✓	
Less VAT may be payable by Jack as a result of operating the scheme	✓	

Task 7.7

	✓
Yes, because output VAT would be paid later and input VAT would be reclaimed at the same time or earlier	✓
No, because input VAT would be reclaimed later and output VAT would be paid at the same time or earlier	

Chapter 8

Task 8.1

B   Less than the error correction reporting threshold and not deliberate

Task 8.2

	True	False
Amy can adjust this on her next return provided she also informs HMRC in writing of the error		✓
Amy cannot adjust this error on her next return and will be liable for a penalty		✓

Task 8.3

	✓
No – not shown on the return	
Yes – shown in box 1	
Yes – shown in box 4	✓

It is shown as an increase in the output tax at box 1 on the VAT return.

Task 8.4

VAT account

Details	Amount £	Details	Amount £
Purchases	4,782.00	Sales	5,265.80
Understated input tax	800.00	Overstated output tax	(700.00)
Purchases returns	(184.20)	Sales returns	(101.00)
Total VAT deductible	5,397.80	Total VAT payable	4,464.80
Less VAT payable	(4,464.80)		
Due from HMRC	933.00		

Standard rated purchases total

£(9,950 + 5,792 + 8,168) = £23,910 × 20% =   £4,782.00

Standard rated purchases returns total

£(178 + 743) = £921 × 20% =   £184.20

Standard rated sales total

£(6,237 + 19,008 + 1,084) = £26,329 × 20% =   £5,265.80

Standard rated sales returns total

£505 × 20% =   £101.00

Task 8.5

B   HMRC will issue a surcharge liability notice

Task 8.6

A business has a requirement to retain VAT records for six years.

Task 8.7

	✓
TRUE	
FALSE	✓

Tax avoidance is a way of trying to legally reduce your tax burden, whereas tax evasion is illegal and consists of seeking to pay too little tax by deliberately misleading HMRC.

Chapter 9

Task 9.1

To: Howard
From: AN Accountant
Date: 1 June 20X0
Subject: VAT deregistration

Please be advised that the current level of your business turnover is such that you are able to VAT   deregister.   As you will no longer need to charge   output   VAT to your customers, there are two options open to you.

(1) Your selling prices can decrease to the VAT-exclusive amount.
    As a result your profits will   stay the same.   At the same time your customer will have   a lower   cost.

(2) Your selling prices can stay at the same VAT-inclusive amount.
    As a result your profits will   increase.   At the same time your customer will have   the same   cost.

If you wish to discuss this further please feel free to make an appointment.

Kind regards

Task 9.2

ABC & Co
2 Smith Street
London
W1 2DE

1 October 20X0

Mr Jones
Unit 1 Alias Industrial Estate,
Chelmsford,
Essex,
CM2 3FG

Dear Mr Jones

Annual accounting scheme

Further to our telephone conversation of today, I have set out below the details relating to the annual accounting scheme.

Your business can join the annual accounting scheme if the value of its taxable supplies **excluding** VAT, in the forthcoming **12** months does not exceed £**1,350,000.**

Under this scheme the business usually makes **nine** equal monthly instalments. Each of these instalments is **1/10** of the estimated VAT liability. The first payment is due at the **end** of the **fourth** month of the accounting period.

The balancing payment and the VAT return will be sent to HMRC within **two months** of the end of the accounting period.

I hope that this has clarified the position. If you wish to discuss this further please do not hesitate to contact me.

Yours sincerely

SAMPLE ASSESSMENT
INDIRECT TAX

Time allowed: 1.5 hours

SAMPLE ASSESSMENT

Sample Assessment

Section 1

This section is about applying your knowledge of VAT and using reference material to make recommendations or decisions.

Task 1.1

(a) **You have the following information about the taxable supplies of three businesses. For each of them, indicate whether they need to register for VAT immediately, or monitor turnover and register later. Tick ONE box on EACH line.**

		Register now	Monitor and register later
A	A new business with an expected turnover of £6,500 per month for the next 12 months		
B	An existing business with a total turnover of £71,500 for the last 11 months. Sales for the next 30 days are not yet known.		
C	An existing business with a total turnover of £6,500 per month for the last 12 months.		

(b) **Choose ONE reason why a business making taxable supplies might choose to register for VAT voluntarily.**

    A   Preparation of VAT returns would be optional
    B   Customers would benefit by being able to claim back input VAT
    C   The business would benefit by being able to claim back input VAT

Task 1.2

(a) **A sales invoice for taxable supplies is being processed. What will be the effect on VAT? Choose ONE answer.**

    A   Input tax will increase.
    B   Input tax will decrease.
    C   Output tax will increase.
    D   Output tax will decrease.

(b) **A business supplies goods that are a mixture of standard-rated and zero-rated. Which of the following statements is true? Choose ONE answer.**

A   All of the input VAT can be reclaimed.

B   None of the input VAT can be reclaimed.

C   All of the input VAT can be reclaimed providing certain (*de minimis*) conditions are met.

D   Some of the input VAT can be reclaimed, in proportion to the different types of supply.

(c) **A business raises a pro forma invoice and receives a payment in advance of making a supply. The pro forma invoice was dated 3 March X0. The payment was received on 10 March X0. The goods were supplied on 14 March X0 and the VAT invoice was raised on 17 March X0. What is the tax point? Choose ONE answer.**

A   3 March X0
B   10 March X0
C   14 March X0
D   17 March X0

Task 1.3

A retail business that receives most of its sales in cash and buys most of its purchases on credit has an estimated turnover for the next 12 months of £760,000.

(a) **What is the turnover limit for eligibility to join the cash accounting scheme? Choose ONE answer.**

A   Estimated turnover in the next 12 months not more than £1,350,000
B   Estimated turnover in the next 12 months not more than £1,600,000

(b) **Is the business eligible to join the cash accounting scheme? Choose ONE answer.**

A   Yes
B   No

(c) **Would the cash accounting scheme improve the cash flow of this business? Choose ONE answer.**

A   Yes, because they would be able to reclaim input VAT earlier
B   Yes, because they would pay output VAT later
C   No, because they would reclaim input VAT later
D   No, because they would pay output VAT earlier

Task 1.4

(a) You have the following extract from a manufacturing business's cash payments during the last month. Select either Yes or No in the right-hand box to show whether the input VAT can be reclaimed on the next VAT return.

Description	£ net	£ VAT	£ Total	Reclaim input VAT?
Office supplies	150.00	30.00	180.00	**Yes / No**
Purchase of company car	9,500.00	1,900.00	11,400.00	**Yes / No**
Computer	450.00	90.00	540.00	**Yes / No**
Entertaining UK business clients	130.00	26.00	156.00	**Yes / No**

(b) You discover that a purchase invoice has been entered in a business's records twice and so the VAT has been reclaimed twice for the quarter ended 31 December X0. The amount of VAT is £185.90 and you are about to prepare the VAT return for the quarter ended 31 March X1. The Box 6 figure on the last VAT return was £180,000. What action should you take? Choose ONE answer.

A   Ignore the error as it is less than 1% of the Box 6 figure for the quarter ended 31 December X0

B   Add £185.90 to the Box 4 figure for the VAT return for the quarter ended 31 March X1

C   Deduct £185.90 from the Box 4 figure for the VAT return for the quarter ended 31 March X1

D   Obtain and complete form VAT 652 "Notification of Errors in VAT Returns"

Task 1.5

(a) A business makes a taxable supply at the standard rate of 20%. The value of the supply is £800. A trade discount of 15% is applied and a settlement discount of 1.5% is offered. What is the correct amount of VAT to be shown on the invoice? Choose ONE answer.

A   £133.96
B   £136.00
C   £157.60
D   £160.00

(b) You have received a supplier credit note. What affect will this have on the amount of VAT due to HMRC? Choose ONE answer.

A   The amount payable will increase
B   The amount payable will decrease

Section 2

Task 2.1

This task is about preparing figures for a VAT Return for a business for the period ended 31 March 20X0.

The standard rate of VAT is 20%.

The business's EU acquisitions are goods that would normally be standard-rated.

The following accounts have been extracted from the business's ledgers.

Sales and sales return account

Date 20X0	Reference	Debit £	Date 20X0	Reference	Credit £
01/01-31/03	Sales returns day-book-UK sales returns	9,000.00	01/01-31/03	Sales day-book -UK sales	670,000.00
31/03	Balance c/d	759,200.00	01/01-31/03	Sales day-book -EU despatches	98,200.00
	Total	768,200.00		Total	768,200.00

Purchases account

Date 20X0	Reference	Debit £	Date 20X0	Reference	Credit £
01/01-31/03	Purchases day-book - UK purchases	311,000.00	31/03	Balance c/d	357,000.00
01/01-31/03	Purchases day-book - EU acquisitions	12,000.00			
01/01-31/03	Purchases day-book - zero-rated imports	34,000.00			
	Total	357,000.00		Total	357,000.00

VAT account

Date 20X0	Reference	Debit £	Date 20X0	Reference	Credit £
01/01-31/03	Sales returns day-book	1,800.00	01/01-31/03	Sales day-book	134,000.00
01/01-31/03	Purchases day-book	62,200.00			

(a) **Calculate the figure for VAT due on acquisitions from other EC member states.**

£ [ ]

(b) **Calculate the figure for Box 1 of the VAT Return - VAT due on sales and other outputs.**

£ [ ]

(c) **Calculate the figure for Box 4 of the VAT Return - VAT reclaimed on purchases and other inputs, including acquisitions from the EC.**

£ [ ]

Task 2.2

This task is about completing a VAT Return for a business for the quarter ended 31 August 20X0.

The following accounts have been extracted from the business's ledgers.

Sales account

Date	Reference	Debit £	Date	Reference	Credit £
31/08/X0	Balance c/d	600,600.00	01/06/X0-31/08/X0	Sales day-book -UK sales	572,600.00
			01/06/X0-31/08/X0	Sales day-book -EU despatches	28,000.00
	Total	600,600.00		Total	600,600.00

Purchases account

Date	Reference	Debit £	Date	Reference	Credit £
01/06/X0-31/08/X0	Purchases day-book -UK purchases	230,800.00	31/08/X0	Balance c/d	271,800.00
01/06/X0-31/08/X0	Purchases day-book -zero-rated imports	41,000.00			
	Total	271,800.00		Total	271,800.00

VAT account

Date	Reference	Debit £	Date	Reference	Credit £
01/06/X0-31/08/X0	Purchases day-book	46,160.00	01/06/X0-31/08/X0	Sales day-book	114,520.00

You are also told that bad debt relief of £4,200.00 is to be claimed in this quarter.

Complete boxes 1 to 9 of the VAT return for the quarter ended 31 August 20X0.

VAT Return for quarter ended 31 August 20X0		£
VAT due in this period on sales and other outputs	Box 1	
VAT due in this period on acquisitions from other EC Member States	Box 2	
Total VAT due (the sum of boxes 1 and 2)	Box 3	
VAT reclaimed in the period on purchases and other inputs including acquisitions from the EC	Box 4	
Net VAT to be paid to HM Revenue & Customs or reclaimed by you (Difference between boxes 3 and 4)	Box 5	
Total value of sales and all other outputs excluding any VAT Include your box 8 figure	Box 6	
Total value of purchases and all other inputs excluding any VAT Include your box 9 figure	Box 7	

Total value of all supplies of goods and related costs excluding any VAT to other EC Member states	Box 8	
Total value of all acquisitions of goods and related costs excluding any VAT from other EC Member states	Box 9	

Task 2.3

You are an accounting technician for a business reporting to the financial accountant.

You have completed the following VAT Return for the quarter ended 31 March 20X0.

VAT Return for quarter ended 31 March 20X0		£
VAT due in this period on sales and other outputs	Box 1	142,371.25
VAT due in this period on acquisitions from other EC Member states	Box 2	11,340.00
Total VAT due (the sum of boxes 1 and 2)	Box 3	153,711.25
VAT reclaimed in the period on purchases and other inputs including acquisitions from the EC	Box 4	57,785.00
Net VAT to be paid to HM Revenue & Customs or reclaimed by you (Difference between boxes 3 and 4)	Box 5	95,926.25
Total value of sales and all other outputs excluding any VAT include your box 8 figure	Box 6	859,450
Total value of purchases and all other inputs excluding any VAT include your box 9 figure	Box 7	395,000
Total value of all supplies of goods and related costs excluding any VAT to other EC Member states	Box 8	45,900
Total value of all acquisitions of goods and related costs excluding any VAT from other EC Member states	Box 9	64,800

The business does not operate any special accounting schemes.

Today's date is 20 April 20X0.

Draft an email to the financial accountant advising her of the amount of VAT that will be paid or received and the date due.

To: _____ (**Financial Accountant / Accounting Technician / HMRC**)

From: _____ (**Financial Accountant / Accounting Technician / HMRC**)

Date: _____ (**31 March 20X0 / 20 April 20X0 / 30 April 20X0**)

Subject:
Completed VAT Return

Please be advertised that I have completed the VAT Return for the quarter ended _____ (**31 March 20X0 / 20 April 20X0 / 30 April 20X0 / 7 May 20X0**)

The amount of VAT_____ (**receivable / payable**) will be £_____.

_____

(**Please arrange to pay this electronically to arrive no later than 30 April 20X0 /
Please arrange to pay this electronically to arrive no later than 7 May 20X0 /
Please arrange to pay this electronically to arrive no later than 31 May 20X0 /
Please expect to see this as a receipt in our bank account**)

Kind regards

Please delete as appropriate.

SAMPLE ASSESSMENT
INDIRECT TAX

ANSWERS

Sample Assessment answers

Section 1

Task 1.1

(a) A   Monitor and register later.

      B   Monitor and register later.

      C   Register now.

(b) C   A is not factually correct; once registered, even voluntarily, the same rules apply as to compulsory registration. B is not correct because VAT-registered customers would neither gain nor lose because they could reclaim VAT charged to them, and non-registered customers would be disadvantaged because they would be charged VAT they could not reclaim.

Task 1.2

(a) C   Output tax will increase.

(b) A   All of the input VAT can be reclaimed (because all of the supplies are taxable. It would be different if some of the supplies were exempt).

(c) B   10 March X0 (because the date of payment is before the date of supply or the date of the invoice).

Task 1.3

(a) A   Estimated turnover in the next 12 months not more than £1,350,000

(b) A   Yes

(c) C   No, because they would reclaim input VAT later

Task 1.4

(a)   Office supplies – Yes

Company car – No

Computer – Yes

Entertaining UK business clients – No

(b)   C   Deduct £185.90 from the Box 4 figure for the VAT return for the quarter ended 31 March X1. A is wrong as an error should never be ignored; the 1% threshold applies to whether the error can be rectified on the return or should be notified separately, not to whether the error should be corrected at all. B would duplicate the error and D is not required as the error is less than £10,000 which itself is greater than 1% of the Box 6 figure (ie £1,800).

Task 1.5

(a)   A   £133.96 (VAT is calculated on the amount net of trade and settlement discount, regardless of whether the settlement discount is taken ie £800 – 15% – 1.5% × 20% = £133.96).

(b)   A   The amount payable will increase.

Section 2

Task 2.1

(a) Calculate the figure for VAT due on acquisitions from other EC member states.

£ | 2,400

(b) Calculate the figure for Box 1 of the VAT Return - VAT due on sales and other outputs.

£ | 132,200 | (£134,000.00 - £1,800)

(c) Calculate the figure for Box 4 of the VAT Return - VAT reclaimed on purchases and other inputs, including acquisitions from the EC,

£ | 64,600 | (£62,200 + £2,400)

Task 2.2

Complete boxes 1 to 9 of the VAT Return for the quarter ended 31 August 20X0.

VAT Return for the quarter ended 31 August 20X0		£
VAT due in this period on sales and other outputs	Box 1	114,520.00
VAT due in this period on acquisitions from other EC Member States	Box 2	0
Total VAT due (the sum of boxes 1 and 2)	Box 3	114,520.00
VAT reclaimed in the period on purchases and other inputs, including acquisitions from the EC	Box 4	50,360.00
Net VAT to be paid to HM Revenue & Customs or reclaimed by you (Difference between boxes 3 and 4)	Box 5	64,160.00
Total value of sales and all other outputs excluding any VAT Include your box 8 figure	Box 6	600,600
Total value of purchases and all other inputs excluding any VAT Include your box 9 figure	Box 7	271,800

| Total value of all supplies of goods and related costs, excluding any VAT, to other EC Member States | Box 8 | 28,000 |
| Total value of all acquisitions of goods and related costs, excluding any VAT, from other EC Member States | Box 9 | 0 |

Task 2.3

Draft an email to the financial accountant advising her of the amount of VAT that will be paid or received and the date due.

To: Financial Accountant

From: Accounting Technician

Date: 20 April 20X0

Subject:
Completed VAT Return

Please be advertised that I have completed the VAT Return for the quarter ended | 31 March 20X0

The amount of VAT | payable | will be £ | 95,926.25

Please arrange to pay this electronically to arrive no later than 7 May 20X0

Kind regards

PRACTICE ASSESSMENT 1
INDIRECT TAX

Time allowed: 1.5 hours

Indirect Tax Practice Assessment 1

Section 1

This section is about applying your knowledge of VAT and using reference material to make recommendations or decisions.

Task 1.1

(a) Joseph makes zero-rated supplies and Julie makes standard-rated supplies. Both are considering voluntarily registering for VAT. Julie's customers are mostly VAT-registered themselves.

Identify whether the following statements are True or False (insert a tick).

	True	False
Joseph will be in a repayment position if he voluntarily registers		
Julie's customer's will not suffer the impact of her charging VAT unless they are not VAT- registered		

(b) Clover Ltd has been trading for 12 months. You have extracted the following information in relation to the company. The VAT registration threshold is £73,000.

Turnover	VAT excl £
Standard-rated	56,000
Zero-rated	11,000
Exempt	8,000

Identify whether the following statement is True or False (insert a tick).

	True	False
Assuming Clover Ltd was not VAT-registered from starting to trade Clover Ltd must VAT register as total turnover exceeds £73,000		

Task 1.2

Adam is a VAT-registered trader making standard-rated supplies. On 19 March 20X0 he received an order from a customer together with a 10% deposit including VAT of £40. The goods were sent out to the customer on 22 March 20X0. An invoice was sent out on 1 April 20X0 that included VAT of £400. The customer paid the balance of the invoice (including VAT of £360) on 30 April 20X0.

Calculate the amount of output tax to be included on Adam's VAT return to:

(a) **31 March 20X0**

    A   Nil
    B   £40
    C   £360
    D   £400

(b) **30 June 20X0**

    A   Nil
    B   £40
    C   £360
    D   £400

Task 1.3

Igor has been trading for many years and makes standard-rated supplies. He is in the flat rate scheme. The flat rate percentage that he must use is 10.5%.

In the latest quarter, Igor had total turnover of £9,000 excluding VAT. He also had VAT-exclusive purchases of £2,000.

(a) **Identify which one of the following is the output tax figure to be included in Igor's VAT return.**

    A   £945.00
    B   £1,134.00
    C   £882.00

(b) **In this quarter, would Igor have more or less VAT to pay to HMRC if he was not in the flat rate scheme.**

    A   More VAT payable if not in the flat rate scheme
    B   Less VAT payable if not in the flat rate scheme

Task 1.4

(a) You have extracted the following information from the accounting records of a client.

Detail	Net £	VAT £	Gross £
Car (for use by salesman)	14,000.00	2,800.00	16,800.00
Hotels (for sales reps while on business)	2,400.00	480.00	2,880.00
Client lunches	460.00	92.00	552.00

Calculate the total amount of input tax that is recoverable by the client relating to these items of expenditure.

A   £Nil
B   £92.00
C   £480.00
D   £3,372.00

(b) A VAT-registered business makes a mixture of exempt and taxable supplies. Which of the following statements is true? Choose ONE answer.

A   Only the input tax relating to taxable supplies is recoverable, in all circumstances
B   All input tax is recoverable if certain de minimis tests are satisfied
C   No input tax is recoverable
D   All input tax is recoverable as no supplies are outside the scope of VAT

Task 1.5

(a) You have the following information about three businesses with a quarter ended 30 June 20X0. For each of them indicate the date of submission of the VAT return, and the date of payment of any VAT payable.

		VAT return	VAT payment
A	Argo submits paper returns and sends a cheque with his return		
B	Zach submits his returns online and pays electronically		
C	Frances submits her returns online and pays by direct debit		

Narrative:

30 July 20X0
31 July 20X0

7 August 20X0

10 August 20X0

(b) **Which one of the following is not a valid reason for a business making taxable supplies choosing to operate the annual accounting scheme?**

    A   Only one VAT return per annum is required

    B   It helps regulate cash flow

    C   It reduces the administrative burden on the business

    D   Only one VAT payment per annum is required

Section 2 – Preparing a VAT return and communicating VAT information

Tutorial Note: The assessor has indicated that the AAT will most likely present the information within Section 2 of the assessment as quarterly ledger accounts with no monthly analysis, as seen in the Sample Assessment. The three practice assessments within this Question Bank, incorporates the method described above, along with other methods of presenting information (including the method used by the AAT on the previous version of the Sample Assessment). This is to ensure you become familiar with a variety of layouts and feel confident in extracting the correct figures to complete the VAT return.

Task 2.1

The following accounts have been extracted from Company A's ledgers for quarter ended 31 December 20X0.

SALES DAY BOOK SUMMARY

	Zero-rated sales	Standard-rated sales	VAT	Total
UK sales	15,000.00	70,000.00	14,000.00	99,000.00

PURCHASES DAY BOOK SUMMARY

	Zero-rated purchases	Standard-rated purchases	VAT	Total
UK purchases/expenses	2,500.00	17,200.00	3,440.00	23,140.00

PURCHASES RETURNS DAY BOOK SUMMARY

	Standard-rated purchases	VAT	Total
UK purchases	2,300.00	460.00	2,760.00

In December 20X0 two debts were written off as irrecoverable (bad) in Company A's accounting records. The first debt was for £758 on an invoice dated 15 March 20X0; the second was for £622 with an invoice dated 23 August 20X0. Company A's payment terms are strictly 30 days from date of invoice. Both figures are stated inclusive of VAT.

(a) **Calculate the figure to be reclaimed for bad debt relief in the quarter ended 31/12/X0.**

The figure to be reclaimed for bad debt relief is:	

(b) **Calculate the figure for Box 1 of the VAT return quarter ended 31/12/X0.**

The figure for Box 1 of the VAT return is:	

(c) **Calculate the figure for Box 4 of the VAT return quarter ended 31/12/X0.**

The figure for Box 4 of the VAT return is:	

Task 2.2

This task is about completing a VAT return for Company B.

The following details have been extracted from the company's accounting ledgers:

QUARTER ENDED 31 MARCH 20X0

Sales account

Date	Reference	Debit £	Date	Reference	Credit £
			01/01/X0-31/03/X0	Sales day-book -UK sales	797,830.00
31/03/X0	Balance c/d	872,990.00	01/01/X0-31/03/X0	Sales day-book -EU despatches	75,160.00
	Total	872,990.00		Total	872,990.00

Purchases/ expenses account

Date	Reference	Debit £	Date	Reference	Credit £
31/03/X0	Purchases day-book	520,565.00	01/01/X0-31/03/X0	Balance c/d	520,565.00
	Total	520,565.00		Total	520,565.00

VAT account

Date	Reference	Debit £	Date	Reference	Credit £
01/01/X0-31/03/X0	Purchases day-book	104,113.00	01/01/X0-31/03/X0	Sales day-book	159,566.00

A debt of £606, inclusive of VAT, was written-off as irrecoverable (bad) in March 20X0. The related sale was made ten months ago. Bad debt relief is now to be claimed.

Complete boxes 1 to 9 of the VAT return for the quarter ended 31 March 20X0

VAT due in this period on **sales** and other outputs (Box 1)

VAT due in this period on **acquisitions** from other **EC Member States** (Box 2)

Total VAT due (**the sum of boxes 1 and 2**) (Box 3)

VAT reclaimed in the period on **purchases** and other inputs, including acquisitions from the EC (Box 4)

Net VAT to be paid to HM Revenue & Customs or reclaimed by you (**Difference between boxes 3 and 4**) (Box 5)

Total value of **sales** and all other outputs excluding any VAT. **Include your box 8 figure** (Box 6)

Whole pounds only

Total value of purchases and all other inputs excluding any VAT. **Include your box 9 figure** (Box 7)

Whole pounds only

Total value of all **supplies** of goods and related costs, excluding any VAT, to other **EC Member States** (Box 8)

Whole pounds only

Total value of all **acquisitions** of goods and related costs, excluding any VAT, from other **EC Member States** (Box 9)

Whole pounds only

Task 2.3

Sonia Liesl works for Company C, and wants to know how to treat (for VAT purposes) purchases made by Company C from outside the EU.

Write a memo to Sonia Liesl giving her the brief details she requests.

MEMO

To:	Sonia Liesl
From:	An Accountant
Subject:	VAT on imports
Date:	14 April 20X0

Briefly, the rule is that if we ☐ goods from a non-EU country we have to ☐ VAT on import at the ☐ rate on point of entry in to the UK. It will normally be possible to ☐ this as VAT. Hence the net cost to the business is nil

---

Picklist:

import
acquire
despatch
pay
zero
standard
charge
reduced
export
reclaim

PRACTICE ASSESSMENT 1
INDIRECT TAX

ANSWERS

Indirect Tax Practice Assessment 1 – Answers

Section 1

Task 1.1

(a)

	True	False
Joseph will be in a repayment position if he voluntarily registers	✓	
Julie's customer's will not suffer the impact of her charging VAT unless they are not VAT-registered	✓	

(b)

	True	False
Assuming Clover Ltd was not VAT-registered from starting to trade		
Clover Ltd must VAT-register as total turnover exceeds £73,000		✓

Only taxable turnover is considered when determining whether the threshold has been exceeded. Taxable turnover is £67,000.

Task 1.2

(a) **31 March 20X0**

   B   £40

(b) **30 June 20X0**

   C   £360

Task 1.3

(a) B £1,134.00

(£9,000 × 120%) × 10.5% = £1,134.00

(b) A More VAT payable if not in the flat rate scheme

If not in the flat rate scheme Igor's VAT payable would be:

		£
Output tax	£9,000 × 20%	1,800.00
Input tax	£2,000 × 20%	(400.00)
		1,400.00

As this is more than £1,134.00 Igor would have more VAT payable.

Task 1.4

(a) C £480.00

VAT is irrecoverable on cars with an element of private use and on business entertaining.

(b) B All input tax is recoverable if certain de minimis tests are satisfied

Task 1.5

(a)

		VAT return	VAT payment
A	Argo submits paper returns and sends a cheque with his return	31 July 20X0	31 July 20X0
B	Zach submits his returns online and pays electronically	7 August 20X0	7 August 20X0
C	Frances submits her returns online and pays by direct debit	7 August 20X0	10 August 20X0

Note. From 1 April 2010 the date of receipt for VAT paid by cheque will be when cleared funds receive HMRC's bank account. This means that payment must be sent so that it arrives 3 business days before the end of the relevant month. However, HMRC is adopting a lenient approach where the cheque relates to a quarter beginning before 1 April 2010, provided the cheque arrives by the month end.

(b) D Only one VAT payment per annum is required

Section 2 – Preparing a VAT return and communicating VAT information

Task 2.1

(a)

The figure to be reclaimed for bad debt relief is:	£126.33

£758 × 1/6 = £126.33

(b)

The figure for Box 1 of the VAT return is:	£14,000.00

(c) **Calculate the figure for Box 4 of the VAT return.**

The figure for Box 4 of the VAT return is:	£3,106.33

£3,440.00 - £460.00 + £126.33

Task 2.2

VAT due in this period on **sales** and other outputs (Box 1)	159,566.00
VAT due in this period on **acquisitions** from other **EC Member States** (Box 2)	0
Total VAT due (**the sum of boxes 1 and 2**) (Box 3)	159,566.00
VAT reclaimed in the period on **purchases** and other inputs, including acquisitions from the EC (Box 4)	104,214.00
Net VAT to be paid to HM Revenue & Customs or reclaimed by you (**Difference between boxes 3 and 4**) (Box 5)	55,352.00
Total value of **sales** and all other outputs excluding any VAT. **Include your box 8 figure** (Box 6)	872,990

	Whole pounds only
Total value of purchases and all other inputs excluding any VAT. **Include your box 9 figure** (Box 7)	520,565

	Whole pounds only
Total value of all **supplies** of goods and related costs, excluding any VAT, to other **EC Member States** (Box 8)	75,160

	Whole pounds only
Total value of all **acquisitions** of goods and related costs, excluding any VAT, from other **EC Member States** (Box 9)	0

Whole pounds only

Task 2.3

MEMO

To: Sonia Liesl

From: An Accountant

Subject: VAT on imports

Date: 14 April 20X0

Briefly, the rule is that if we **import** goods from a non-EU country, we have to **pay** VAT on import at the **standard** rate on point of entry into the UK. It will normally be possible to **reclaim** this as recoverable VAT. Hence the net cost to the business is nil.

PRACTICE ASSESSMENT 2
INDIRECT TAX

Time allowed: 1.5 hours

Indirect Tax Practice Assessment 2

Section 1

This section is about applying your knowledge of VAT and using reference material to make recommendations or decisions.

Task 1.1

(a) In his previous VAT return Jacob overstated the input tax. He is able to adjust for this on his current VAT return.

What affect will this have on the amount of VAT payable to HMRC this quarter? Choose one answer.

A   The amount payable will increase

B   The amount payable will decrease

(b)

Claudia deliberately understated her output VAT on her last return but now she wishes to correct this.

Identify which one of the following statements is the correct action Claudia must take to correct the error

A   The error can be adjusted for on the next return, but Claudia must also inform HMRC separately and she may be liable to a penalty

B   The error cannot be adjusted on the next return, so Claudia must inform HMRC separately in writing, and will not be liable to a penalty

C   The error cannot be adjusted on the next return, so Claudia must inform HMRC separately in writing, and may also be liable to a penalty

Task 1.2

Identify whether each of the following statements is True or False.

(a) Where a settlement discount is offered, VAT should be calculated based on the discount obtained rather than the full discount offered.

    A   True

    B   False

(b) The VAT fuel scale charge is the amount of input tax recoverable on private fuel purchases.

    A   True

    B   False

(c) When a trader issues a credit note to a customer it decreases the VAT payable by the trader for that quarter.

    A   True

    B   False

Task 1.3

Gomez uses the annual accounting scheme for his business. The business's VAT liability for the year ended 30 June 20X0 was £15,000 and for the following year, the year ended 30 June 20X1 was £18,500.

(a) **The final balancing payment for the year ended 30 June X1 is:**

    A   £Nil

    B   £3,500

    C   £5,000

    D   £18,500

(b) **The final balancing payment is due by:**

    A   30 June 20X1

    B   30 July 20X1

    C   31 July 20X1

    D   31 August 20X1

Task 1.4

(a) Xavier has a quarter ended 31 December 20X0. His normal payment terms are one calendar month after invoice date.

Identify whether bad debt relief can be claimed in respect of the following amounts owed to Xavier as at 31 December 20X0.

Moraira Ltd owes £3,000 from an invoice issued on 2 January 20X0. Xavier believes that the amount will be paid in full and so it has not been written-off in the accounts.

A Bad debt relief can be claimed
B Bad debt relief cannot be claimed.

Calpe Ltd owes £2,000 from an invoice issued on 15 June 20X0. Xavier does not expect that the amount will be paid in and so it has been written-off in the accounts.

A Bad debt relief can be claimed
B Bad debt relief cannot be claimed.

(b) **Where a business can claim bad debt relief, what effect will this have on the amount of VAT payable to HMRC for the quarter? Choose one answer.**

A The amount payable will increase
B The amount payable will decrease

Task 1.5

(a) **Insert the missing figures in the table below.**

Net £	VAT @ 20% £	Gross £
		270.60
260.00		

(b) **Identify whether the following statements in relation to VAT invoices are True or False (insert a tick).**

	True	False
A VAT invoice must include certain details including the VAT registration number, the total VAT payable and a description of the goods supplied		
A less detailed invoice may be issued if the VAT inclusive proceeds are less than £150		
If a sale is made to a VAT registered customer in the EU, the invoice must include the standard rate of VAT unless the invoice includes the customer's VAT number		

Section 2 – Preparing a VAT return and communicating VAT information

Tutorial Note: The assessor has indicated that the AAT will most likely present the information within Section 2 of the assessment as quarterly ledger accounts with no monthly analysis, as seen in the Sample Assessment. The three practice assessments within this Question Bank, incorporates the method described above, along with other methods of presenting information (including the method used by the AAT on the previous version of the Sample Assessment). This is to ensure you become familiar with a variety of layouts and feel confident in extracting the correct figures to complete the VAT return.

Task 2.1

This task is about preparing figures for a VAT Return for a business run by Joseph Marselus for the period ended 31 March 20X0.

The standard rate of VAT is 20%.

The following accounts have been extracted from Joseph's ledgers.

Sales and sales return account

Date 20X0	Reference	Debit £	Date 20X0	Reference	Credit £
01/01-31/03	Sales returns day-book-UK sales returns	13,000.00	01/01-31/03	Sales day-book -UK sales	275,000.00
31/03	Balance c/d	262,000.00			
	Total	275,000.00		Total	275,000.00

Purchases account

Date 20X0	Reference	Debit £	Date 20X0	Reference	Credit £
01/01-31/03	Purchases day-book - UK purchases	101,000.00	31/03	Balance c/d	101,000.00
	Total	101,000.00		Total	101,000.00

VAT account

Date 20X0	Reference	Debit £	Date 20X0	Reference	Credit £
01/01-31/03	Sales returns day-book	2,600.00	01/01-31/03	Sales day-book	55,000.00
01/01-31/03	Purchases day-book	20,200.00			

Joseph Marselus accidentally left out a couple of invoices from his last VAT return.

- Invoice 1 was for £3,400.00 (VAT-exclusive) to a customer
- Invoice 2 was for £254.00 (VAT-exclusive) from a supplier

He is able to correct them on his next return.

(a) For each of the above invoices calculate the VAT adjustment figures to correct these errors.

Invoice 1 £ [   ]

Invoice 2 £ [   ]

(b) Calculate the figure for Box 1 of the VAT Return.

£ [   ]

(c) Calculate the figure for Box 4 of the VAT Return.

£ [   ]

Task 2.2

This task is about completing a VAT return for Gilbert Jones Ltd.

The following details have been extracted from the company's accounting records for the period August to October 20X0.

Sales: UK – standard-rated

Date		Dr £	Cr £
31/08/X0	Sales day-book		185,463.00
30/09/X0	Sales day-book		186,795.00
31/10/X0	Sales day-book		189,674.00
TOTAL			561,932.00

Sales: EU despatches – zero-rated

Date		Dr £	Cr £
31/08/X0	Sales day-book		10,856.00
30/09/X0	Sales day-book		9,745.00
31/10/X0	Sales day-book		8,796.00
TOTAL			**29,397.00**

Purchases: UK – standard-rate

Date		Dr £	Cr £
31/08/X0	Purchases day-book	62,758.00	
30/09/X0	Purchases day-book	64,241.00	
31/10/X0	Purchases day-book	65,913.00	
TOTAL		**192.912.00**	

Purchases: EU acquisitions – standard-rated

Date		Dr £	Cr £
31/08/X0	Purchases day-book	0	
30/09/X0	Purchases day-book	0	
31/10/X0	Purchases day-book	15,400.00	
TOTAL		**15,400.00**	

VAT: Output tax

Date		Dr £	Cr £
31/08/X0	Sales day-book		37,092.60
30/09/X0	Sales day-book		37,359.00
31/10/X0	Sales day-book		37,934.80
TOTAL			**112,386.40**

VAT: Input tax

Date		Dr £	Cr £
31/08/X0	Purchases day-book	12,551.60	
30/09/X0	Purchases day-book	12,848.20	
31/10/X0	Purchases day-book	16,262.60	
TOTAL		**41,662.40**	

Complete boxes 1 to 9 of the business's VAT return for the quarter ended 31 October 20X0.

VAT due in this period on **sales** and other outputs (Box 1)

VAT due in this period on **acquisitions** from other **EC Member States** (Box 2)

Total VAT due (**the sum of boxes 1 and 2**) (Box 3)

VAT reclaimed in the period on **purchases** and other inputs, including acquisitions from the EC (Box 4)

Net VAT to be paid to HM Revenue & Customs or reclaimed by you (**Difference between boxes 3 and 4**) (Box 5)

Total value of **sales** and all other outputs excluding any VAT. **Include your box 8 figure** (Box 6)

Whole pounds only

Total value of purchases and all other inputs excluding any VAT. **Include your box 9 figure** (Box 7)

Whole pounds only

Total value of all **supplies** of goods and related costs, excluding any VAT, to other **EC Member States** (Box 8)

Whole pounds only

Total value of all **acquisitions** of goods and related costs, excluding any VAT, from other **EC Member States** (Box 9)

Whole pounds only

Task 2.3

You are the deputy accountant for Donald Smith Ltd and you have been provided with the following information. It is 12 Nov 20X0.

The Showroom of Donald Smith Ltd sold some goods with a market value of £15,000 to a customer, GHA Stores plc, in February 20X0 on 30 days' credit. Donald Smith Ltd was informed yesterday that GHA Stores plc had ceased trading and the debt is irrecoverable. This is the first time that Donald Smith Ltd has had a substantial bad debt. Donald Smith Ltd has a VAT registration number of 482 912 5407.

You are required to write to HMRC, seeking confirmation of your understanding of the steps that Donald Smith Ltd needs to take in order to claim bad debt relief for the VAT element of this debt, and the timescale in which the steps should be taken so that relief is obtained as soon as possible.

DONALD SMITH LTD

Park Drive Trading Estate, Sunninghill Road, Ascot, Berks GU8 5ZD

Telephone: 01344 627896

VAT Office
Lyle House
Henry Road
Guildford
Surrey
GU8 5CM

12 November 20X0

Dear Sirs

Registration number 482 912 5407

We have recently been informed that a net sale of £_____ to GHA Stores plc in February on 30 days' credit is now a bad debt. Please confirm that the steps set out below will enable us to claim bad debt relief for the VAT element of the debt (£_____) in our next VAT return.

- Write off the entire debt of £_____ in our accounts before 31 January 20X1

- Retain a copy of the VAT invoice and the journal writing it off

- In our next VAT return, for the quarter ending 31 January 20X1 (when the debt will be more than _____ months overdue), add £_____ to Box __ (input tax box).

I look forward to receiving your confirmation. Thank you for your help

Yours faithfully

Deputy Accountant

Picklist:

£3,000

£18,000

£3,600

£21,600

£15,000

£3,000

12

6

1

4

PRACTICE ASSESSMENT 2
INDIRECT TAX

ANSWERS

Indirect Tax Practice Assessment 2 – Answers

Section 1

Task 1.1

(a) A The amount payable will increase

(b) C The error cannot be adjusted on the next return, so Claudia must inform HMRC separately in writing, and may also be liable to a penalty

Task 1.2

(a) B False

The VAT is based on the maximum possible discount

(b) B False

The fuel scale charge is an amount of output tax to offset against the input tax reclaimed on fuel purchase invoices.

(c) A True

A sales credit note decreases the VAT payable

Task 1.3

(a) **The final balancing payment for the year ended 30 June X1 is:**

C   £5,000

£18,500 – (90% × 15,000) paid in instalments.

(b) **The final balancing payment is due by:**

D   31 August 20X1 within 2 months of VAT annual period.

Task 1.4

(a) Moraira Ltd owes £3,000 from an invoice issued on 2 January 20X0. Xavier believes that the amount will be paid in full and so it has not been written-off in the accounts.

B   Bad debt relief cannot be claimed.

The debt has not been written off in the accounts

Calpe Ltd owes £2,000 from an invoice issued on 15 June 20X0. Xavier does not expect that the amount will be paid in and so it has been written-off in the accounts.

B   Bad debt relief cannot be claimed.

It is less than six months since the debt was due for payment (15 July 20X0)

(b)   B   The amount payable will decrease

Task 1.5

(a)   **Insert the missing figures in the table below.**

Net £	VAT @ 20% £	Gross £
225.50	45.10	270.60
260.00	52.00	312.00

£270.60 × 5/6 = £225.50

£260.00 × 20% = £52.00

(b)   **Identify whether the following statements in relation to VAT invoices are True or False (insert a tick).**

	True	False
A VAT invoice must include certain details including the VAT registration number, the total VAT payable and a description of the goods supplied	✓	
A less detailed invoice may be issued if the VAT-inclusive proceeds are less than £150		✓
If a sale is made to a VAT-registered customer in the EU, the invoice must include the standard rate of VAT unless the invoice includes the customer's VAT number	✓	

Section 2 – Preparing a VAT return and communicating VAT information

Task 2.1

(a)

Invoice 1   £ | 680.00

$£3,400 \times 20\%$

Invoice 2   £ | 50.80

$£254 \times 20\%$

(b) **Box 1 of the VAT Return.**

£ | 53,080.00

$£55,000.00 - £2,600.00 + £680.00$

(c) **Box 4 of the VAT Return.**

£ | 20,250.80

$£20,200.00 + £50.80$

Task 2.2

VAT due in this period on **sales** and other outputs (Box 1)

| 112,386.40 |

VAT due in this period on **acquisitions** from other **EC Member States** (Box 2)

| 3,080.00 |

Total VAT due (**the sum of boxes 1 and 2**) (Box 3)

| 115,466.40 |

VAT reclaimed in the period on **purchases** and other inputs, including acquisitions from the EC (Box 4)

| 41,662.40 |

Net VAT to be paid to HM Revenue & Customs or reclaimed by you (**Difference between boxes 3 and 4**) (Box 5)

| 73,804.00 |

Total value of **sales** and all other outputs excluding any VAT. **Include your box 8 figure** (Box 6)

| 591,329 |

Whole pounds only

Total value of purchases and all other inputs excluding any VAT. **Include your box 9 figure** (Box 7)

| 208,312 |

Whole pounds only

Total value of all **supplies** of goods and related costs, excluding any VAT, to other **EC Member States** (Box 8)

| 29,397 |

Whole pounds only

Total value of all **acquisitions** of goods and related costs, excluding any VAT, from other **EC Member States** (Box 9)

| 15,400 |

Whole pounds only

Workings

Box 6	UK sales	561,932.00
	EU sales	29,397.00
		591,329.00

Box 7	Purchases Day book- Purchases	192,912.00
	EU acquisitions	15,400.00
		208,312.00

Task 2.3

DONALD SMITH LTD

Park Drive Trading Estate, Sunninghill Road, Ascot, Berks GU8 5ZD

Telephone 01344 627896

VAT Office
Lyle House
Henry Road
Guildford
Surrey
GU8 5CM

12 November 20X0

Dear Sirs

Registration number 482 912 5407

We have recently been informed that a net sale of **£15,000** to GHA Stores plc in February on 30 days' credit is now a bad debt. Please confirm that the steps set out below will enable us to claim bad debt relief for the VAT element of the debt (**£3,000.00**) in our next VAT return.

- Write off the entire debt of **£18,000.00** in our accounts before 31 January 20X1
- Retain a copy of the VAT invoice and the journal writing it off
- In our next VAT return, for the quarter ending 31 January 20X1 (when the debt will be more than **six** months overdue), add **£3,000.00** to Box **4** (input tax box).

I look forward to receiving your confirmation. Thank you for your help

Yours faithfully

Deputy Accountant

PRACTICE ASSESSMENT 3
INDIRECT TAX

Time allowed: 1.5 hours

Indirect Tax Practice Assessment 3

Section 1

This section is about applying your knowledge of VAT and using reference material to make recommendations or decisions.

Task 1.1

(a)　It is 31 December, Julian has been trading for ten months and his taxable turnover has consistently been £6,500 per month. Next months turnover is expected to be the same.　**Indicate whether Julian should register for VAT immediately or monitor his turnover and register later. (insert a tick)**

	✓
Register immediately	
Monitor turnover and register later	

(b)　It is 31 December, Jasper has been trading for ten months and his taxable turnover has consistently been £5,500 per month. Next month he is expecting a one off payment of £71,000, in addition to his normal monthly turnover.
Indicate whether Julian should register for VAT immediately or monitor his turnover and register later. (Insert a tick)

	✓
Register immediately	
Monitor turnover and register later	

Task 1.2

Identify for the two statements below whether they are True or False (insert a tick).

(a)　When a trader receives a credit note from a supplier VAT payable by the trader will increase.

	✓
TRUE	
FALSE	

(b) A business makes supplies that are both standard-rated and zero-rated. All of the input VAT can be reclaimed providing certain (de minimis) conditions are met.

	✓
TRUE	
FALSE	

(c) A registered trader receives an order for goods on 15 June 20X1. The trader delivers the goods to the customer on 20 June 20X1, and issues an invoice on 23 June 20X1. The customer pays for the goods in full on 2 July 20X1.

Identify the tax point for this transaction (insert a tick).

	✓
15 June 20X1	
20 June 20X1	
23 June 20X1	
2 July 20X1	

Task 1.3

(a) A business operates the cash accounting scheme

Indicate which one of the following statements would be a benefit of using this scheme (insert a tick).

	✓
Only having to submit one VAT return a year	
Automatic bad debt relief	
Paying a percentage of turnover over to HMRC	

(b) A business operates the annual accounting scheme.

Indicate which one of the following statements would be a correct when using this scheme (insert a tick).

	✓
Each year, the business submits one annual return and makes one payment	
Each year, the business submits one annual return and makes ten payments	
Each year, the business submits one annual return and makes four payments	

(c)   A business operates the flat rate scheme.

Indicate which one of the following statements would be a correct when using this scheme (insert a tick).

	✓
The business pays a percentage of tax-inclusive turnover to HMRC and reclaims input VAT	
The business pays a percentage of tax-exclusive turnover to HMRC and reclaims input VAT	
The business pays a percentage of tax-inclusive turnover to HMRC and cannot reclaim input VAT	
The business pays a percentage of tax-exclusive turnover to HMRC and cannot reclaim input VAT	

Task 1.4

(a)   Vince is an employee of Brown Ltd and he has the use of a company car which he uses both privately and for business. Brown Ltd pays for all the petrol costs on the car which amount to £725 (including VAT) for the quarter.   The VAT fuel scale charge for this car for the quarter is £89.33

Complete the following showing how much output VAT must be paid to cover the private use of the car, and how much input VAT (if any) can be reclaimed for the petrol costs.

	£
Output tax	
Input tax	

(b)   Victoria made an error on her last VAT return. She needs to inform HMRC in writing preferably by completing form 652 "Notification of Errors in VAT Returns".

Identify with a tick any of the following statements that could be correct in relation to this error

	✓
The error is less than the error correction reporting threshold, but deliberate	
The error is less than the error correction reporting threshold, but not deliberate	
The error is more than the error correction reporting threshold, and deliberate	

The error is more than the error correction reporting threshold, but not deliberate	

Task 1.5

(a)   Rocco received the following VAT-exclusive invoice from a supplier

Goods	£2,500.00
Less trade discount 15%	(£375.00)
	£2,125.00

There was an additional 5% discount if payment was made within 30 days. Rocco did not take this discount up

Identify with a tick how much VAT should be shown on the invoice.

	✓
£500.00	
£425.00	
£403.75	
£354.16	

(b)   **Identify with a tick which TWO of the follow does not need to be included on a valid VAT invoice.**

	✓
VAT number of supplier	
Invoice date	
VAT number of customer	
Rate of VAT	
Total price excluding VAT	
Total amount of VAT	
Total price including VAT	
Name and address of customer	
Name and address of supplier	

Section 2 – Preparing a VAT return and communicating VAT information

Tutorial Note: The assessor has indicated that the AAT will most likely present the information within Section 2 of the assessment as quarterly ledger accounts with no monthly analysis, as seen in the Sample Assessment. The three practice assessments within this Question Bank, incorporates the method described above, along with other methods of presenting information (including the method used by the AAT on the previous version of the Sample Assessment). This is to ensure you become familiar with a variety of layouts and feel confident in extracting the correct figures to complete the VAT return.

Task 2.1

This task is about preparing figures for a VAT Return for the business of Guy LeBlond.

The standard rate of VAT is 20%.

The business's EU acquisitions are goods that would normally be standard-rated.

The following accounts have been extracted from Guy's accounts over a three month period .

SALES DAY BOOK SUMMARY

	Zero-rated sales	Standard-rated sales	VAT	Total
UK sales	42,500.00	567,000.00	113,400.00	722,900.00

PURCHASES DAY BOOK SUMMARY

	Zero-rated purchases	Standard-rated purchases	VAT – on UK purchases	EU acquisitions	Total
UK purchases/expenses	4,250.00	150,600.00	30,120.00	25,678.00	210,648.00

(a) **Calculate the figure for Box 1 of the VAT Return.**

£ [   ]

(b) **Calculate the figure for Box 2 of the VAT Return.**

£ [   ]

(c) **Calculate the figure for Box 4 of the VAT Return.**

£ [   ]

Task 2.2

This task is about completing a VAT return.

The following accounts have been extracted from Bradley Ltd's ledgers for quarter ended 30 June 20X1.

SALES DAY BOOK SUMMARY

	Zero-rated sales	Standard-rated sales	VAT	Total
UK sales	22,500.00	67,000.00	13,400.00	102,900.00

PURCHASES DAY BOOK SUMMARY

	Zero-rated purchases	Standard-rated purchases	VAT	Total
UK purchases/expenses	4,250.00	15,600.00	3,120.00	22,970.00

SALES RETURNS DAY BOOK SUMMARY

	Standard-rated sales	VAT	Total
UK Sales	3,700.00	740.00	4,440.00

CASH PAYMENTS BOOK SUMMARY

	Net	VAT	Total
Cash purchases/expenses	8,550.00	1,710.00	10,260.00

JOURNAL (extract)

	Debit	Credit
	£	£
Irrecoverable (bad) debts expense	5,200.00	
VAT account	1,040.00	
Receivables (debtors) (VAT inclusive at 20 %)		6,240.00

Complete boxes 1 to 9 of the VAT return for quarter ended 30 June 20X1

VAT due in this period on sales and other outputs (Box 1)

VAT due in this period on acquisitions from other EC Member States (Box 2)

Total VAT due (the sum of boxes 1 and 2) (Box 3)

VAT reclaimed in the period on purchases and other inputs, including acquisitions from the EC (Box 4)

Net VAT to be paid to HM Revenue & Customs or reclaimed by you (Difference between boxes 3 and 4) (Box 5)

Total value of sales and all other outputs excluding any VAT. Include your box 8 figure (Box 6)

Whole pounds only

Total value of purchases and all other inputs excluding any VAT. Include your box 9 figure (Box 7)

Whole pounds only

Total value of all supplies of goods and related costs, excluding any VAT, to other EC Member States (Box 8)

Whole pounds only

Total value of all acquisitions of goods and related costs, excluding any VAT, from other EC Member States (Box 9)

Task 2.3

Reply to Holly Field's email giving her the information she has requested

To: Accounts assistant

From: Holly Field

Subject: Impact of a rise in the VAT rate

Date: 17 July 20X1

I have been listening to the news recently and have heard there may be a rise in the standard rate of VAT from 20% to 25%.

I am extremely concerned as to how this will affect my business. Most of my sales are direct to the general public, so I am unsure whether to increase my prices to take account of the proposed new rate, or to try and keep them the same.

Would you mind explaining the consequences of these two options for me?

Your speedy response would be much appreciated,

Holly

You are required to reply to Holly, filling in the missing details of the email below.

EMAIL

To:	Holly Field
From:	Accounts assistant
Subject:	Impact of a rise in the VAT rate
Date:	20 July 20X1

Dear Holly,

Thank you for your email requesting details of how the proposed rise in the standard rate of VAT might affect your business.

As you quite rightly say, you _____, which means effectively, you as a business will suffer the impact of the increased rate. Alternatively you could _____, resulting in your customers having to pay extra, which in itself, may lead to the loss of revenue.

For example with the present rate of VAT at 20% if you want to make income of £100 on a sale you will charge your customers _____.

With a proposed rise to 25% you can either:

- _____ to your customer, which will still leave you £100; or

- _____ for your customers, leaving you only £96 after output VAT is charged. (£120 × 100/125).

This is a decision that you will need to give careful thought to, but I hope this helps clarifies the situation for you,

Kind regards,

Accounts Assistant

Picklist:

could keep your prices the same

increase your prices

£100.

£120.

charge £125 (£100 plus 25% VAT)

keep your price at £120

PRACTICE ASSESSMENT 3
INDIRECT TAX

ANSWERS

Indirect Tax Practice Assessment 3 – Answers

Section 1

Task 1.1

(a)

	✔
Register immediately	
Monitor turnover and register later	✓

(b)

	✔
Register immediately	✓
Monitor turnover and register later	

Task 1.2

(a) When a trader receives a credit note from a supplier the input VAT recoverable will decrease resulting in the VAT payable increasing.

	✔
TRUE	✓
FALSE	

(b) The de minimis test is applied when a trader makes taxable and *exempt* supplies. A business that makes supplies that are standard-rated and zero-rated (both taxable supplies) can reclaim all its input without applying any tests.

	✔
TRUE	
FALSE	✓

(c) The basic tax point (delivery date) of 20 June is replaced by the actual tax point (invoice date) of 23 June as the invoice is issued within 14 days of the basic tax point.

	✓
15 June 20X1	
20 June 20X1	
23 June 20X1	✓
2 July 20X1	

Task 1.3

(a) A business operating the cash accounting scheme will benefit from:

	✓
Only having to submit one VAT return a year	
Automatic bad debt relief	✓
Paying a percentage of turnover over to HMRC	

(b) When a **business operates the annual accounting scheme:**

	✓
Each year, the business submits one annual return and makes one payment	
Each year, the business submits one annual return and makes ten payments	✓
Each year, the business submits one annual return and makes four payments	

(c) **When a business operating the flat rate scheme:**

	✓
The business pays a percentage of tax-inclusive turnover to HMRC and reclaims input VAT	
The business pays a percentage of tax-exclusive turnover to HMRC and reclaims input VAT	
The business pays a percentage of tax-inclusive turnover to HMRC and cannot reclaim input VAT	✓
The business pays a percentage of tax-exclusive turnover to HMRC and cannot reclaim input VAT	

Task 1.4

(a) Brown Ltd can reclaim all the VAT on petrol costs as input VAT (ie £725 ×1/6) for the quarter, but must pay output VAT based on the relevant fuel scale charge.

	£
Output tax	89.33
Input tax	120.83

(b)

	✓
The error is less than the error correction reporting threshold, but deliberate	✓
The error is less than the error correction reporting threshold, but not deliberate	
The error is more than the error correction reporting threshold, and deliberate	✓
The error is more than the error correction reporting threshold, but not deliberate	✓

Task 1.5

(a) The VAT will always be worked out on the figure after deducted all possible discounts, even if they are not taken up. £2,125.00 × 95% × 20% = £403.75

	✓
£500.00	
£425.00	
£403.75	✓
£354.16	

(b)

	✓
VAT number of supplier	
Invoice date	
VAT number of customer	✓
Rate of VAT	
Total price excluding VAT	
Total amount of VAT	
Total price including VAT	✓
Name and address of customer	
Name and address of supplier	

Section 2 – Preparing a VAT return and communicating VAT information

Task 2.1

(a) **Box 1 of the VAT Return..**

£ | 113,400.00 |

(b) **Box 2 of the VAT Return.**

£ | 5,135.60 |

£25,678.00 × 20%

(c) **Box 4 of the VAT Return.**

£ | 35,255.60 |

£30,120.00 + £5,135.60

Task 2.2

VAT due in this period on sales and other outputs (Box 1)	12,660.00
VAT due in this period on acquisitions from other EC Member States (Box 2)	0
Total VAT due (the sum of boxes 1 and 2) (Box 3)	12,660.00
VAT reclaimed in the period on purchases and other inputs, including acquisitions from the EC (Box 4)	5,870.00
Net VAT to be paid to HM Revenue & Customs or reclaimed by you (Difference between boxes 3 and 4) (Box 5)	6,790.00
Total value of sales and all other outputs excluding any VAT. Include your box 8 figure (Box 6)	85,800

	Whole pounds only
Total value of purchases and all other inputs excluding any VAT. Include your box 9 figure (Box 7)	28,400

	Whole pounds only
Total value of all supplies of goods and related costs, excluding any VAT, to other EC Member States (Box 8)	0

	Whole pounds only
Total value of all acquisitions of goods and related costs, excluding any VAT, from other EC Member States (Box 9)	0

Whole pounds only

Workings

		£
Box 1	Sales day book	13,400.00
	Sales returns day book	(740.00)
		12,660.00
Box 4	Purchases day book	3,120.00
	Cash payments book	1,710.00
	Bad debt relief	1,040.00
		5,870.00
Box 6	Sales day book —standard rated	67,000.00
	Sales day book – zero rated	22,500.00
	Sales returns day book	(3,700.00)
		85,800.00

Box 7	Purchases day book – standard rated	15,600.00
	Purchases day book – zero-rated	4,250.00
	Cash payments book	8,550.00
		28,400.00

Task 2.3

EMAIL

To:	Holly Field
From:	Accounts assistant
Subject:	Impact of a rise in the VAT rate
Date:	20 July 20X1

Dear Holly,

Thank you for your email requesting details of how the proposed rise in the standard rate of VAT might affect your business.

As you quite rightly say, you **could keep your prices the same**, which means effectively, you as a business will suffer the impact of the increased rate. Alternatively you could **increase your prices**, resulting in your customers having to pay extra, which in itself, may lead to the loss of revenue.

For example with the present rate of VAT at 20% if you want to make income of £100 on a sale you will charge your customers **£120.**

With a proposed rise to 25% you can either:

- **charge £125 (£100 plus 25% VAT)** to your customer, which will still leave you £100; or

- **keep your price at £120** for your customers, leaving you only £96 after output VAT is charged. (£120 × 100/125).

This is a decision that you will need to give careful thought to, but I hope this helps clarifies the situation for you,

Kind regards,

Accounts Assistant

INDEX

Accounting Qualification

Indirect Tax (Level 3)
Reference material

The Association of Accounting Technicians
September 2011

Reference material for AAT assessment of Indirect Tax

Introduction

This document comprises data that you may need to consult during your Indirect Tax computer-based assessment.

The material can be consulted during the practice and live assessments through pop-up windows. It is made available here so you can familiarise yourself with the content before the test.

Do not take a print of this document into the exam room with you*.

This document may be changed to reflect periodical updates in the computer-based assessment, so please check you have the most recent version while studying.

*Unless you need a printed version as part of reasonable adjustments for particular needs, in which case you must discuss this with your tutor at least six weeks before the assessment date.

Contents   Page

2

Introduction to VAT

VAT is a tax that's charged on most goods and services that VAT-registered businesses provide in the UK. It's also charged on goods and some services that are imported from countries outside the European Union (EU), and brought into the UK from other EU countries.

VAT is charged when a VAT-registered business sells to either another business or to a non-business customer. This is called output tax.

When a VAT-registered business buys goods or services for business use it can generally reclaim the VAT it has paid. This is called input tax.

Her Majesty's Revenue and Customs (HMRC) is the government department responsible for operating the VAT system. Payments of VAT collected are made by VAT-registered businesses to HMRC.

3

Rates of VAT

There are three rates of VAT, depending on the goods or services the business provides. The rates are:
- standard – 20%. The standard-rate VAT fraction is 20/120 or 1/6
- reduced - 5%. The reduced rate VAT fraction is 5/105
- zero - 0%

There are also some goods and services that are:
- exempt from VAT
- outside the UK VAT system altogether

Taxable supplies

If you sell zero-rated goods or services, they count as taxable supplies, but you don't add any VAT to your selling price because the VAT rate is 0%.

If you sell goods or services that are exempt, you don't charge any VAT and they're not taxable supplies. This means that you won't normally be able to reclaim any of the VAT on your expenses.

Generally, you can't register for VAT or reclaim the VAT on your purchases if you sell only exempt goods or services. If you sell some exempt goods or services you may not be able to reclaim the VAT on all of your purchases.

If you buy and sell only - or mainly - zero-rated goods or services you can apply to HM Revenue & Customs to be exempt from registering for VAT. This could make sense if you pay little or no VAT on your purchases.

4

Registration and deregistration limits

Supplying goods or services within the UK

If, at the end of any month, your turnover of VAT taxable goods and services (taxable turnover) supplied within the UK for the previous 12 months is more than the current registration threshold of £73,000, you must register for VAT without delay. You must also register if, at any time, you expect the value of your taxable turnover in the next 30 day period alone to go over the registration threshold..

If your trading is below the threshold for registration

If your taxable turnover hasn't crossed the registration threshold, you can still apply to register for VAT voluntarily.

Deregistration threshold

The deregistration threshold is £71,000. If your taxable turnover for the year is less than or equal to £71,000, or if you expect it to fall to £71,000 or less in the next 12 months, you can either:

- stay registered for VAT, or
- ask for your VAT registration to be cancelled

5

Keeping business records and VAT records

If you are registered for VAT, you must keep certain business records and VAT records.

You do not have to keep these records in a set way - just so your records:

- are complete and up to date
- allow you to work out correctly the amount of VAT you owe to HMRC or can reclaim from HMRC
- are easily accessible when HMRC visits you, eg the figures you use to fill in your VAT Return must be easy to find

Business records

Business records you need to keep include the following:

- annual accounts, including profit and loss accounts
- bank statements and paying-in slips
- cash books and other account books
- orders and delivery notes
- purchase and sales books
- records of daily takings such as till rolls
- relevant business correspondence

In addition to these business records, you need to keep VAT records and a VAT account.

VAT records

In general, you must keep the following VAT records:

- Records of all the standard-rated, reduced rate, zero-rated and exempt goods and services that you buy or sell.
- Copies of all sales invoices you issue. However, if you are a retailer you do not have to keep copies of any less detailed (simplified) VAT invoices for items under £250 including VAT
- All purchase invoices for items you buy.
- All credit notes and debit notes you receive.
- Copies of all credit notes and debit notes you issue.
- Records of any goods or services bought for which you cannot reclaim the VAT, such as business entertainment.
- Records of any goods you export.
- Any adjustments, such as corrections to your accounts or amended VAT invoices.
- A VAT account

For how long must VAT records be kept?

Generally you must keep all your business records that are relevant for VAT for at least six years. If this causes you serious problems in terms of storage or costs, then HMRC may allow you to keep some records for a shorter period.

Keeping a VAT account

A VAT account is the separate record you must keep of the VAT you charged on your sales (output VAT or VAT payable) and the VAT you paid on your purchases (input VAT or VAT reclaimable). It provides the link between your business records and your VAT Return. You need to add up the VAT in your sales and purchases records and then transfer these totals to your VAT account, using separate headings for VAT payable and VAT reclaimable.

You can keep your VAT account in whatever way suits your business best, as long as it includes information about the VAT that you:

6

- owe on your sales
- owe on acquisitions from other European Union (EU) countries
- owe following a correction or error adjustment
- can reclaim on your business purchases
- can reclaim on acquisitions from other EU countries
- can reclaim following a correction or error adjustment
- are reclaiming via VAT bad debt relief

You must also keep records of any adjustments that you make, such as balancing payments if you use annual accounting for VAT.

You can use the information from your VAT account to complete your return at the end of each accounting period. You subtract your VAT reclaimable from your VAT payable, to give the net amount of VAT you pay to or reclaim from HMRC.

Unless you are using the cash accounting scheme, you must pay the VAT you have charged customers during the accounting period that relates to the return, even if they have not paid you.

7

Exempt and partly-exempt businesses

Exempt goods and services

There are some goods and services on which VAT is not charged.

Exempt supplies are not taxable for VAT. So you do not include sales of exempt goods or services in your taxable turnover for VAT purposes. If you buy exempt items, there is no VAT to reclaim.

This is different to zero-rated supplies. In both cases VAT is not added to the selling price, but zero-rated goods or services are taxable for VAT at 0%.

If you only sell or supply exempt goods or services

If you only sell or otherwise supply goods or services that are exempt from VAT then your business is an exempt business. You cannot register for VAT - so you won't be able to reclaim any VAT on your purchases.

This is in contrast to the situation if you sell or otherwise supply zero-rated goods or services, where you can reclaim the VAT on any purchases that relate to those sales. In addition, if you sell mainly or only zero-rated items, you may apply for an exemption from VAT registration, but then you can't claim back your input tax.

Reclaiming VAT in a partly exempt business

If you are registered for VAT but make some exempt supplies your business is partly exempt.
Generally, you won't be able to reclaim the input VAT you've paid on purchases that relate to your exempt supplies.

If the amount of input VAT incurred relating to exempt supplies is below a minimum 'de minimus' amount, input VAT can be reclaimed in full.

If the amount of input VAT incurred relating to exempt supplies is above the 'de minimus' amount, only the part of the input VAT that related to non-exempt supplies can be reclaimed.

8

Tax points

The time of supply, known as the 'tax point', is the date when a transaction takes place for VAT purposes. This date is not necessarily the date the supply physically takes place.

Generally, you must pay or reclaim VAT in the VAT period in which the time of supply occurs (usually quarterly), and use the correct rate of VAT in force on that date. This means you'll need to know the time of supply/tax point for every transaction so you can put it on the right VAT Return.

Time of supply (tax point) for goods and services

The time of supply for VAT purposes is defined as follows.
- For transactions where no VAT invoice is issued (for example, sales to customers who aren't registered for VAT), the time of supply is normally the date the supply physically takes place (as defined below).
- For transactions where there is a VAT invoice, the time of supply is normally the date the invoice is issued, even if this is before or after the date the supply physically took place (as defined below). To issue a VAT invoice, you must send (by post, email etc) or give it to your customer for them to keep. A tax point cannot be created simply by preparing an invoice.

However there are exceptions to these rules on time of supply, detailed below.

Date the supply physically takes place

For goods, the time when the goods are considered to be supplied for VAT purposes is the date when one of the following happens.
- The supplier sends the goods to the customer.
- The customer collects the goods from the supplier.
- The goods (which are not either sent or collected) are made available for the customer to use, for example if the supplier is assembling something on the customer's premises.

For services, the date when the services are considered to be supplied for VAT purposes is the date when the service is carried out and all the work - except invoicing - is finished.

Exceptions regarding time of supply (tax point)

The above general principles for working out the time of supply do not apply in the following situations.

- For transactions where a VAT invoice is issued or payment is received in advance, the time of supply is the date the payment is received or the date the invoice is issued - whichever is the earlier.

- If the supplier receives full payment before the date when the supply takes place and no VAT invoice has yet been issued, the time of supply is the date the payment is received.

- If the supplier receives part-payment before the date when the supply takes place, the time of supply becomes the date the part-payment is received but only for the amount of the part-payment (assuming no VAT invoice has been issued before this date - in which case the time of supply is the date the invoice is issued). The time of supply for the remainder will follow the normal rules - and might fall in a different VAT period, and so have to go onto a different VAT Return.

- If the supplier issues a VAT invoice more than 14 days after the date when the supply took place, the time of supply will be the date the supply took place, and not the date the invoice is issued. However, if a supplier has genuine commercial difficulties in invoicing within 14 days of the supply taking place, they can contact HM Revenue & Customs (HMRC) to ask whether they can have permission to issue invoices later than 14 days and move the time of supply to this later date.

9

VAT invoices

What is a VAT invoice?

A VAT invoice shows certain VAT details of a sale or other supply of goods and services. It can be either in paper or electronic form.

A VAT-registered customer must have a valid VAT invoice from the supplier in order to claim back the VAT they have paid on the purchase for their business.

What is NOT a VAT invoice?

The following are not VAT invoices:
- pro-forma invoices
- invoices for only zero-rated or exempt supplies
- invoices that state 'this is not a tax invoice'
- statements
- delivery notes
- orders
- letters, emails or other correspondence

You cannot reclaim the VAT you have paid on a purchase by using these documents as proof of payment.

What a VAT invoice must show

A VAT invoice must show:
- an invoice number which is unique and follows on from the number of the previous invoice - if you spoil or cancel a serially numbered invoice, you must keep it to show to a VAT officer at your next VAT inspection
- the seller's name or trading name, and address
- the seller's VAT registration number
- the invoice date
- the time of supply or tax point if this is different from the invoice date
- the customer's name or trading name, and address
- a description sufficient to identify the goods or services supplied to the customer

For each different type of item listed on the invoice, you must show:
- the unit price or rate, excluding VAT
- the quantity of goods or the extent of the services
- the rate of VAT that applies to what's being sold
- the total amount payable, excluding VAT
- the rate of any cash or settlement discount
- the total amount of VAT charged

If you issue a VAT invoice that includes zero-rated or exempt goods or services, you must:
- show clearly that there is no VAT payable on those goods or services
- show the total of those values separately

You may round down the total VAT payable on all goods and services shown on a VAT invoice to a whole penny. You can ignore any fraction of a penny. (This concession is not available to retailers.)

Time limits for issuing VAT invoices

There is a strict time limit on issuing VAT invoices. You must normally issue a VAT invoice (to a VAT-registered customer) within 30 days of the date you supply the goods or services – or, if you were paid in advance, the date you received payment. This is so your customer can claim back the VAT on the supply, if they're entitled to.

You can't issue invoices any later without permission from HM Revenue & Customs (HMRC) except in a few limited circumstances.

10

You need a valid VAT invoice to reclaim VAT

Even if you are registered for VAT, you can normally only reclaim VAT on your purchases if:
- you buy an item and use it for business purposes and
- you have a valid VAT invoice for the purchase

Only VAT-registered businesses can issue valid VAT invoices. You cannot reclaim VAT on any goods or services that you buy from a business that is not VAT-registered.

11

Where simplified (less detailed) VAT invoices can be issued

Simplified VAT invoices

If you make retail sales and you make a taxable supply of goods or services for £250 or less **including VAT**, then when a customer asks for a VAT invoice, you can issue a simplified (less detailed) VAT invoice that only needs to show:

- the seller's name and address
- the seller's VAT registration number
- the time of supply (tax point)
- a description of the goods or services

Also, if the supply includes items at different VAT rates then for each different VAT rate, your simplified VAT invoice must also show:

- the total price including VAT
- the VAT rate applicable to the item

Exempt supplies must not be included on a simplified VAT invoice.

If you accept credit cards, then you can create a simplified invoice by adapting the sales voucher you give the cardholder when you make the sale. It must show the information described in the six bullets above.

You do not need to keep copies of any less detailed invoices you issue.

Pro-forma invoices

If you need to issue a sales document for goods or services you haven't supplied yet, you can issue a 'pro-forma' invoice or a similar document to offer goods or services to customers.

A pro-forma invoice is not a VAT invoice, and you should clearly mark it with the words "This is not a VAT invoice".

If your potential customer accepts the goods or services you're offering them and if you actually supply them, then you'll need to issue a VAT invoice within the appropriate time limit.

If you have been issued with a pro-forma invoice by your supplier, you can't use that to claim back VAT on the purchase. You must obtain a VAT invoice from your supplier.

Advance payments and deposits

An advance payment, or deposit, is a proportion of the total selling price that a customer pays before you supply them with goods or services. If you ask for an advance payment, the tax point is whichever of the following happens first:

- the date you issue a VAT invoice for the advance payment
- the date you receive the advance payment

You include the VAT on the advance payment on the VAT Return for the period when the tax point occurs.

If the customer pays you the remaining balance before the goods are delivered or the services are performed, another tax point is created when whichever of the following happens first:

- you issue a VAT invoice for the balance
- you receive payment of the balance

So you include the VAT on the balance on the VAT return for the period when the tax point occurs.

Discounts on goods and services

If any of your goods or services are discounted, you charge VAT on the discounted price rather than the full price.

12

If you make an offer to a customer such as 'we will pay your VAT', VAT is actually payable to HM Revenue & Customs (HMRC) on the amount the customer would have paid on the discounted price, not the amount they have paid at the full price.

Returned goods, credit notes, debit notes and VAT

For a buyer who has received a VAT invoice

If you have returned goods to the seller for a full or partial credit you have three options:
- you can return the invoice to your supplier and obtain a replacement invoice showing the proper amount of VAT due, if any
- you can obtain a credit note or supplementary VAT invoice from your supplier
- you can issue a debit note to your supplier

If you issue a debit note or receive a credit note, you must:
- record this in your accounting records
- on your next VAT Return, deduct the VAT on the credit or debit note from the amount of VAT you can reclaim

For a seller who has issued a VAT invoice

If you receive returned goods from a customer, you have three options:
- you can cancel and recover the original invoice, and issue a replacement showing the correct amount of any VAT due, if any
- you can issue a credit note or supplementary VAT invoice to your customer
- you can obtain a debit note from your customer

If you issue a credit note or receive a debit note, you must:
- record this in your accounting records
- on your next VAT Return, deduct the VAT on the credit or debit note from the amount of your VAT payable

13

Business entertainment

Generally you cannot reclaim VAT on business entertainment expenses. Business entertainment is any form of free or subsidised entertainment or hospitality to non-employees.

You can reclaim VAT on employee expenses and entertainment expenses if those expenses relate to travel and subsistence or where you entertain only employees.

When you entertain both employees and non-employees, you can only reclaim VAT on the proportion of the expenses that is for employees.

14

Cars and motoring expenses

When you buy a car you generally can't reclaim the VAT. There are some exceptions - for example, when the car is used mainly as one of the following:
- a taxi
- for driving instruction
- for self-drive hire

If you couldn't reclaim the VAT on the original purchase price of a car you bought new, you won't have to charge any VAT when you sell it. This is because the sale of the car is exempt for VAT purposes. If you did reclaim the VAT when you bought the car new, you charge VAT when you come to sell it.

VAT-registered businesses can generally reclaim the VAT when they buy a commercial vehicle such as a van, lorry or tractor.

Reclaiming VAT on road fuel

If your business pays for road fuel, you can deal with the VAT charged on the fuel in one of four ways:
- Reclaim all of the VAT. You must use the fuel only for business purposes.
- Reclaim all of the VAT and pay the appropriate fuel scale charge - this is a way of accounting for output tax on fuel that your business buys but that's then used for private motoring.
- Reclaim only the VAT that relates to fuel used for business mileage. You'll need to keep detailed records of your business and private mileage.
- Don't reclaim any VAT. This can be a useful option if your mileage is low and also if you use the fuel for both business and private motoring. If you choose this option you must apply it to all vehicles including commercial vehicles.

15

Transactions outside the UK

Exports, despatches, supplying goods abroad: charging VAT

If you sell, supply or transfer goods out of the UK to someone in another country you may need to charge VAT on them.

Generally speaking, you can zero-rate supplies exported outside the European Union (EU, previously known as the European Community or EC), or sent to someone who's registered for VAT in another EU country, provided you follow strict rules, obtain and keep the necessary evidence, and obey all laws.

If you supply goods to another EU country these sales are technically known as despatches (or 'removals') rather than exports. The term 'exports' is reserved to describe sales to a country outside the EU.

VAT on sales to someone who is not VAT registered in another EU country

When you supply goods to someone in another EU country, and they're not registered for VAT in that country, you should normally charge VAT.

VAT on sales to someone who is VAT registered in another EU country

If you're supplying goods to someone who is registered for VAT in the destination EU country, you can zero-rate the supply for VAT purposes, provided you meet certain conditions.

VAT on exports of goods to non-EU countries

VAT is a tax charged on goods used in the European Union (EU), so if goods are exported outside the EU VAT isn't charged. You can zero-rate the supply.

Imports and purchases of goods from abroad: paying and reclaiming VAT

Generally speaking, VAT is payable on all purchases of goods that you buy from abroad at the same rate that would apply to the goods if supplied in the UK. You must tell HMRC about goods that you import, and pay any VAT and duty that is due.

VAT on goods from EU countries

If you are registered for VAT in the UK and receive goods from inside the EU, these are known as acquisitions (or 'arrivals') rather than imports. You must enter the value of the acquisition in Box 9 and Box 7 of your VAT Return and account for VAT in Box 2 of your VAT return using the same rate of VAT that would apply if the goods were supplied in the UK. This VAT is known as acquisition tax. You can reclaim the VAT as if the goods were supplied in the UK by including the same figure in Box 4, subject to the normal VAT rules for reclaiming input tax.

VAT on imports of goods from non-EU countries

VAT may be charged on imports of goods that you buy from non- EU countries. You can reclaim any VAT paid on the goods you have imported as input tax.

16

Bad debts

When you can reclaim VAT on bad debts

You can reclaim VAT that you paid to HM Revenue & Customs and which you have not received from the customer. The conditions are that:
- the debt is more than six months old and less than three years and six months old
- you have written off the debt in your VAT account and transferred it to a separate bad debt account
- the debt has not been sold or handed to a factoring company
- you did not charge more than the normal selling price for the items

How to claim bad debt relief

If you are entitled to claim bad debt relief, you add the amount of VAT you are reclaiming to the amount of VAT you are reclaiming on your purchases (input tax) and put the total figure in Box 4 of your VAT return.

To work out how much bad debt relief you can claim on a VAT-inclusive balance, you need to apply the VAT fraction to the unpaid amount.

17

Submitting returns and paying VAT

You must submit your VAT Return and pay any VAT you owe by the due date.

Paper returns

If you submit a paper return, the due date is usually one month after the end of the VAT period, which is usually quarterly. You can find the date that your return is due printed on the return.

If you submit a paper return and pay it electronically, you can get up to seven extra calendar days after the standard due date shown on your return for payment to reach HMRC. You don't get those seven extra days in the exceptional cases listed below.

Online returns

It is mandatory for all VAT-registered traders with a turnover of £100,000 or more, plus any newly registered traders (regardless of turnover), to submit their returns online and pay electronically.

Therefore most VAT-registered businesses have to submit online VAT Returns and pay electronically. You get seven extra calendar days after the standard due date to submit your online return and to pay any VAT due electronically unless one of the exceptional cases listed below applies to you.

Exceptions to the seven day extension

You do not qualify for the seven extra days after the standard due date to submit your return or make payment if:

- you use the VAT Annual Accounting Scheme
- you are required to make payments on account (unless you submit monthly returns)

VAT payment deadlines

You are responsible for calculating how much VAT you owe and for paying VAT on time. Paying on time will help you avoid having to pay a surcharge.

If you submit an online return you must pay your VAT electronically. If you submit a paper return, you can either pay electronically or enclose payment with your return.

For both online and paper returns, any VAT you owe must have cleared to HMRC's bank account on time whether paid electronically or by cheque.

In most cases, paying electronically provides you with up to seven extra calendar days after your standard due date for cleared funds to reach HM Revenue & Customs' (HMRC's) bank account The exception to this is payment by Direct Debit, when HMRC will automatically collect payment from your bank account three bank working days after the extra seven calendar days following your standard due date.

If you miss the payment deadline you may be liable to a surcharge for late payment.

18

Special accounting schemes

Annual Accounting Scheme for VAT

Using standard VAT accounting, you must complete four VAT Returns each year. Any VAT due is payable quarterly, and any VAT refunds due to you are also repayable quarterly.

Using annual VAT accounting, you usually make nine interim payments at monthly intervals. You only need to complete one return at the end of the year when you either make a balancing payment or receive a balancing refund. Annual accounting can reduce your paperwork and make it easier to manage your cash flow.

You can use annual accounting if your estimated taxable turnover during the next tax year is not more than £1.35 million. If you are already using annual accounting you can continue to do so until your estimated taxable turnover exceeds £1.6 million.

Benefits of annual accounting

- You only need to complete one VAT Return per year, instead of four.
- You get two months rather than one month to complete and send in your annual VAT return and pay the balance of your VAT payable.
- You can better manage your cash flow by paying a fixed amount in monthly instalments.
- You can make additional payments as and when you wish.
- You can join from the day you register for VAT, or if you are already registered.

Disadvantages of annual accounting

- If you regularly reclaim VAT, you will only get one repayment per year.
- If your turnover decreases, your interim payments may be higher than your VAT payments would be under the standard VAT accounting - you would have to wait until the end of the year to receive your refund.

Cash accounting scheme for VAT

Using standard VAT accounting, you pay VAT on your sales whether or not your customer has paid you. Using cash accounting, you do not need to pay VAT until your customer has paid you. If your customer never pays you, you never have to pay the VAT.

You can use cash accounting if your estimated taxable turnover during the next tax year is not more than £1.35 million.

You can continue to use cash accounting until your taxable turnover exceeds £1.6 million.

The benefits of cash accounting

Using cash accounting may help your cash flow, especially if your customers are slow payers. You do not need to pay VAT until you have received payment from your customers, so if a customer never pays you, you don't have to pay VAT on that bad debt as long as you continue to use the cash accounting scheme.

Disadvantages of cash accounting

Using cash accounting may affect your cash flow:
- You cannot reclaim VAT on your purchases until you have paid your suppliers. This can be a disadvantage if you buy most of your goods and services on credit.
- If you regularly reclaim more VAT than you pay, you will usually receive your repayment later under cash accounting than under standard VAT accounting, unless you pay for everything at the time of purchase.
- If you start using cash accounting when you start trading, you will not be able to reclaim VAT on most start up expenditure, such as initial stock, tools or machinery, until you have actually paid for those items.

19

- If you leave the cash accounting scheme you will have to account for all outstanding VAT due, including any bad debts.

Flat rate schemes for VAT

If your taxable turnover is less than £150,000 per year, you could simplify your VAT accounting by calculating your VAT payments as a percentage of your total VAT-inclusive turnover. Although you cannot reclaim VAT on purchases - it is taken into account in calculating the flat rate percentage - the flat rate scheme can reduce the time that you need to spend on accounting for and working out your VAT. Even though you still need to show a VAT amount on each sales invoice, you don't need to record how much VAT you charge on every sale in your accounts. Nor do you need to record the VAT you pay on every purchase.

Benefits of using a flat rate scheme

Using the flat rate scheme can save you time and smooth your cash flow. It offers these benefits:
- You don't have to record the VAT that you charge on every sale and purchase, as you would with standard VAT accounting. This can mean you spending less time on the books, and more time on your business. You do need to show VAT separately on your invoices, just as you do for standard VAT accounting.
- A first year discount. If you are in your first year of VAT registration you get a 1% reduction in your flat rate percentage until the day before the first anniversary you became VAT registered.
- Fewer rules to follow. You no longer have to work out what VAT on purchases you can and can't reclaim.
- Peace of mind. With less chance of mistakes, you have fewer worries about getting your VAT right.
- Certainty. You always know what percentage of your takings you will have to pay to HM Revenue & Customs.

Potential disadvantages of using a flat rate scheme

The flat rate percentages are calculated in a way that takes into account zero-rated and exempt sales. They also contain an allowance for the VAT you spend on your purchases. So the VAT Flat Rate Scheme might not be right for your business if:
- you buy mostly standard-rated items, as you cannot generally reclaim any VAT on your purchases
- you regularly receive a VAT repayment under standard VAT accounting
- you make a lot of zero-rated or exempt sales

20

Errors

Action you must take at the end of your VAT accounting period

At the end of your VAT accounting period, calculate the net value of all the errors you have found during the period that relate to returns you have already submitted - that is, add together any additional tax due to HM Revenue & Customs (HMRC), and subtract any tax you should have claimed back. Don't include any deliberate errors - these must be separately disclosed to HMRC.

What you do next depends on whether the net value of all the errors is less than or greater than the 'error correction reporting threshold'.

The error reporting threshold is the greater of:

- £10,000
- 1% of the box 6 figure on your VAT Return for the period when you discover the error - subject to an upper limit of £50,000

If the net value of all the errors is less than the threshold then, if you prefer, you may correct the errors by making an adjustment on your current VAT Return.

However, if the value of the net VAT errors discovered is above this threshold, you must report them to HMRC separately, in writing.

How to adjust your VAT Return: Method 1

You can correct certain errors whose net value is below the error correction reporting threshold by adjusting your VAT Return.

At the end of the VAT period when you discover the errors, adjust your VAT account of output tax due or input tax claimed by the net amount of all errors. Make sure that your VAT account shows the amount of the adjustment you make to your VAT Return.

If you discovered more than one error, use the net value of all the errors to adjust your return. Adjust box 1 or box 4, as appropriate. For example, if you discover that you didn't account for VAT payable to HMRC of £100 on a supply that you made in the past, and also didn't account for £60 VAT reclaimable on a purchase, add £40 to your box 1 figure on your return.

How to separately report an error to HMRC: Method 2

For certain errors you must separately report to your relevant HMRC VAT Error Correction Team in writing about the mistake. The simplest way to tell them is to use Form VAT 652 "Notification of Errors in VAT Returns", which is for reporting errors on previous returns, but you don't have to use Form VAT 652 - you can simply write a letter instead.

You may, if you wish, use this method for errors of any size which are below the error reporting threshold instead of a Method 1 error correction. If you use this method you must not make adjustment for the same errors on a later VAT return.

You must always use Method 2 if the net errors exceed the error reporting threshold or if the errors made on previous returns were made deliberately.

Surcharges, penalties and assessments

Surcharges if you miss a VAT Return or VAT payment deadlines

You must submit your VAT Return and pay any VAT by the due date. If HM Revenue & Customs (HMRC) receives your return or VAT payment after the due date, you are 'in default' and may have to pay a surcharge in addition to the VAT that you owe.

The first time you default, you will be sent a warning known as a 'Surcharge Liability Notice'. This tells you that if you pay late ('default') again during the following 12 months - known as your surcharge period - you may be charged a surcharge.

If you submit or pay late again during your surcharge period you may have to pay a 'default surcharge'. This is a percentage of your unpaid VAT. If you don't submit a correct return, HMRC will estimate the amount of VAT you owe and base your surcharge on that amount (known as an assessment – see below).

HMRC assessments

You have a legal obligation to submit your VAT Returns and pay any VAT you owe to HMRC by the due date. If you don't submit a return HMRC can issue an assessment which shows the amount of VAT that HMRC believes you owe, based on their best estimate.

Penalties for careless and deliberate errors

Careless and deliberate errors will be liable to a penalty, whether they are adjusted on the VAT return or separately reported.

If a person discovers an error which is neither careless nor deliberate, HMRC expects that they will take steps to correct it. If the person does not take steps to correct it, the inaccuracy will be treated as careless and a penalty will be due.

Penalties for inaccurate returns

You may be liable to a penalty if your VAT Return is inaccurate, and correcting this means tax is unpaid, understated, over-claimed or under-assessed. Telling HMRC about inaccuracies as soon as you are aware of them may reduce any penalty that is due, in some cases to zero.

Penalties for submitting a VAT Return on paper instead of online

If you send your VAT Return on paper when you are required to submit your return online you will be charged a penalty.

Penalty for late registration
If you don't register for VAT with HM Revenue & Customs at the right time then you may be liable to a late registration penalty.

22

Finding out more information about VAT

Most questions can be answered by referring to the HMRC website.

VAT Helpline

If you can't find the answer to your question on the HMRC website, the quickest and easiest way is to ring the VAT Helpline where you can get most of your VAT questions answered. Before you ring, make sure you have your VAT registration number and postcode to hand. If you're not VAT registered you'll need your postcode.

What you can write to HMRC about

The VAT Helpline can answer most questions relating to VAT, but there may be times when you need to write to HMRC.

You can write to HMRC about VAT if:

- you've looked at the VAT information published by HMRC - either on the website or in printed notices and information sheets - and can't find the answer to your question
- you've already contacted the VAT Helpline and they've asked you to write
- you can show that you have real doubt about how VAT affects a particular transaction and your personal situation or business

If HMRC already publishes information that answers your question, they'll write to you and give the relevant details.

23

Visits by VAT officers

VAT officers are responsible for the collection of VAT for the government. They check businesses to make sure that their VAT records are up to date. They also check that amounts claimed from or paid to the government are correct. They examine VAT records, question the business owner or the person responsible for the VAT records and watch business activity.

Before a visit, HMRC will confirm the following details with you:
- the person the VAT officer wants to see
- a mutually convenient appointment date and time
- the name and contact number of the officer carrying out the visit
- which records the officer will need to see, and for which tax periods
- how long the visit is likely to take
- any matters you are unsure of, so that the officer can be better prepared to answer your queries

HMRC will confirm all the above information in writing unless the time before the visit is too short to allow it. They will almost always give you seven days notice of any visit unless you want an earlier one, for example to get your claim paid more quickly.

24

Notes

Notes

REVIEW FORM

How have you used this Text?
(Tick one box only)

☐ Home study

☐ On a course_____

☐ Other _____

Why did you decide to purchase this Text?
(Tick one box only)

☐ Have used BPP Texts in the past

☐ Recommendation by friend/colleague

☐ Recommendation by a college lecturer

☐ Saw advertising

☐ Other _____

During the past six months do you recall seeing/receiving either of the following?
(Tick as many boxes as are relevant)

☐ Our advertisement in Accounting Technician

☐ Our Publishing Catalogue

Which (if any) aspects of our advertising do you think are useful?
(Tick as many boxes as are relevant)

☐ Prices and publication dates of new editions

☐ Information on Text content

☐ Details of our free online offering

☐ None of the above

Your ratings, comments and suggestions would be appreciated on the following areas of this Text.

	Very useful	Useful	Not useful
Introductory section	☐	☐	☐
Quality of explanations	☐	☐	☐
How it works	☐	☐	☐
Chapter tasks	☐	☐	☐
Chapter Overviews	☐	☐	☐
Test your learning	☐	☐	☐
Index	☐	☐	☐
Question / Answer Banks	☐	☐	☐
Practice assessments	☐	☐	☐

	Excellent	Good	Adequate	Poor
Overall opinion of this Text	☐	☐	☐	☐

Do you intend to continue using BPP Products?   ☐ Yes   ☐ No

Please note any further comments and suggestions/errors on the reverse of this page. The publishing manager of this edition can be e-mailed at: ambercottrell@bpp.com

Please return to: Amber Cottrell, Tax Publishing Manager, BPP Learning Media Ltd, FREEPOST, London, W12 8BR.

REVIEW FORM (continued)

TELL US WHAT YOU THINK

Please note any further comments and suggestions/errors below.